Beaded Allure

beadweaving patterns for 25 romantic projects

Kelly Wiese

NORTH LIGHT BOOKS
Cincinnati, Ohio

14 13 12 11   5 4 3

Distributed in Canada by Fraser Direct
100 Armstrong Avenue
Georgetown, ON, Canada L7G 5S4
Tel: (905) 877-4411

Distributed in the U.K. and Europe by
David & Charles, Brunel House, Newton Abbot,
Devon, TQ12 4PU, England
Tel: (+44) 1626 323200, Fax: (+44) 1626 323319
E-mail: postmaster@davidandcharles.co.uk

Distributed in Australia by Capricorn Link
P.O. Box 704, S. Windsor, NSW 2756 Australia
Tel: (02) 4577-3555

Library of Congress Cataloging-in-Publication Data
Wiese, Kelly.
 Beaded allure : beadweaving patterns for 25 romantic projects / by Kelly Wiese. -- 1st ed.
 p. cm.
 Includes index.
 ISBN 978-1-60061-768-3 (pbk. : alk. paper)
 1. Beadwork--Patterns. 2. Weaving--Patterns. 3. Jewelry making. I. Title.
 TT860.W594 2010
 745.594'2--dc22
 2009042187

www.fwmedia.com

Editor: Julie Hollyday
Designer: Rachael Smith and Marissa Bowers
Production Coordinator: Greg Nock
Photographer: Ric Deliantoni
Wardrobe Stylist: Monica Skrzelowski
Makeup and Hair Styling: Gina Weathersby

North Light Books would like to thank Baker Hunt Art and Cultural Center for the generous use of their grounds and buildings. Readers can visit Baker Hunt online at www.bakerhunt.com.

METRIC CONVERSION CHART

TO CONVERT	TO	MULTIPLY BY
Inches	Centimeters	2.54
Centimeters	Inches	0.4
Feet	Centimeters	30.5
Centimeters	Feet	0.03
Yards	Meters	0.9
Meters	Yards	1.1
Sq. Inches	Sq. Centimeters	6.45
Sq. Centimeters	Sq. Inches	0.16
Sq. Feet	Sq. Meters	0.09
Sq. Meters	Sq. Feet	10.8
Sq. Yards	Sq. Meters	0.8
Sq. Meters	Sq. Yards	1.2
Pounds	Kilograms	0.45
Kilograms	Pounds	2.2
Ounces	Grams	28.3
Grams	Ounces	0.035

DEDICATION

This book is dedicated to:

My husband, Paul. Without his love and support, I wouldn't have made it past the beginning stages, let alone to the finished project.

My mom and dad. They nurtured my creativity from such an early age and have always been there for me.

My dear friend Virginia. Without her friendship and encouragement, I wouldn't be where I am today.

I love you all!

ACKNOWLEDGMENTS

From my humble bead beginnings to my bead store to my current designing career, I have had a lot of great times and made a lot of friends. If I hadn't been encouraged and supported by my friends and others along the way, this book wouldn't have been possible. I would like to thank Tonia Davenport, my acquisitions editor, for giving me this wonderful opportunity; she saw my designs at a bead show and took a chance on me. Thanks also to Julie Hollyday, my editor, for her endless patience and encouragement. And thanks to photographer Christine Polomsky; without her help, I would never have figured out how to take the step-by-step photos! In addition, I would like to thank Betcey Ventrella from Beyond Beadery and Beki Haley from Out On a Whim for their great selections of beads, which provided me with so much inspiration.

ABOUT THE AUTHOR

Kelly Wiese is a beadwork designer who teaches beadweaving nationally. Her work has been published in several magazines. Several galleries have also featured her award-winning work. For about eight years, she ran her own bead store in Pueblo, Colorado. She now resides in Fort Morgan, Colorado, with her husband, three dogs and two cats, where she spends as much time as possible playing with beads.

Introduction

When I was a little girl, my dad gave me a bead loom set that he had used as a young boy. I was fascinated with the glass tubes full of tiny beads. There were patterns in bold colors on graph paper and instructions for fobs and lanyards. I never did quite figure out how to make any of the projects on the loom at that time, but it piqued my interest.

Years later, I saw a pair of beaded earrings in a boutique. I couldn't afford the earrings, but I knew I could figure out how to make a pair if I could just find the beads and maybe a book or pattern.

And so it began—my love of beads. Throughout the years, I've gone from student to teacher to bead shop owner and then designer. I've met wonderful people who have shared their knowledge and friendship as I've walked my path. One in particular, Eleanor, introduced me to beadweaving and helped fuel my passion through her time and knowledge.

The opportunity to write this book is a dream come true for me: I get to share my passion and love of beads. I want to spread the joy! The designs presented in this book are meant to evoke a spirit of quiet passion, a romance I've had with beads for most of my life. You'll find familiar techniques shaped into stunning necklaces, bracelets and earrings that showcase grace and femininity. It's my hope that you fall in love, too.

Take your time reviewing the techniques and patterns; get comfortable with the colors (or choose your own to suit your favorite palette); run your fingers through the beautiful beads; then be prepared to make breathtaking jewelry. There is a great feeling of accomplishment when you can wear something that you have made with your own two hands. I truly think beadweaving is good for the soul. How can a person not be happy when surrounded by beautiful beads!

Beadweaving Basics

Every romance has a beginning.
For beadweaving, it's getting to know
the intimate details of tools and materials,
stitches and techniques. The information in
this chapter will help you get comfortable with
the basic items you'll need to help build your own
beadweaving story.

There are endless variations of beadweaving. I tend to
lean toward using certain stitches and techniques, ones that
give my work a romantic or vintage feel, so I've featured
them in this section. Many projects use a combination
of techniques, and if you understand the basics, it makes
learning something new a little easier.

HOW THIS BOOK WORKS

As mentioned above, the projects in this book use a
variety of beadweaving stitches and embellishments, all tied
together in pretty necklaces, bracelets and earrings. While
you follow the instructions for the projects, you'll notice
the steps are the patterns. Bulky and confusing bead charts
are banned from our delicate world. I'll show you step-by-
step and bead-by-bead how these lovely creations are made.
You'll soon find you don't need bead charts anyway—you're
learning how to create your own romance with beads.

Tools and Materials

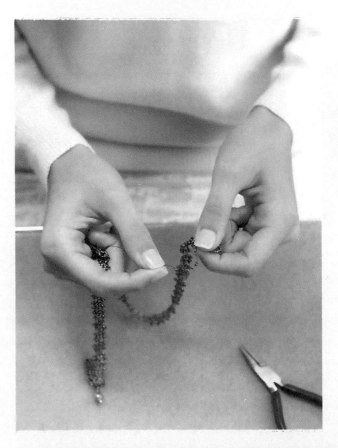

A great thing about beadweaving is that it doesn't require a lot of expensive tools and materials. I encourage you to experiment with the different threads, needles and materials that are available until you find the ones that you like best. Ask any experienced beader and you will find that each one has favorites that she swears by!

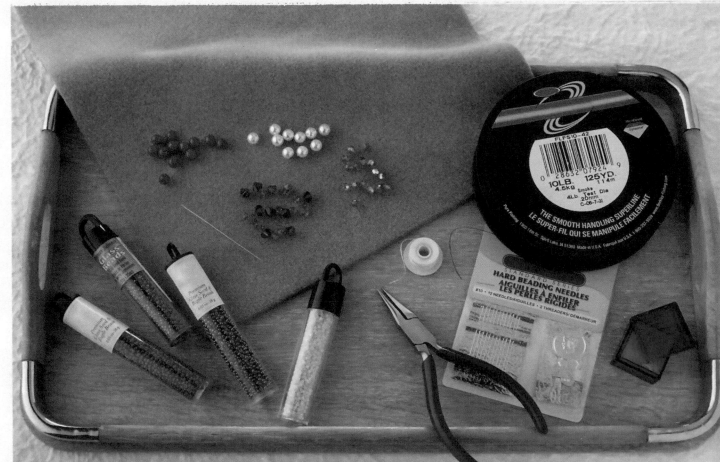

THREAD

There are several different types of beading thread to choose from. I prefer **Nymo Size D** (Nymo comes in a variety of sizes). It is an inexpensive nylon thread that comes in a wide range of colors. Size D is fairly strong but thin enough to get several passes of thread easily through size 11 and size 15 Japanese seed beads.

FireLine is another option. It comes in several different weights and several colors. It is great for working with crystals and other beads that have sharp edges.

One-G is a thread from TOHO Beads out of Japan. It is a little more expensive than Nymo. It does come in a nice selection of colors. I have found it to be easy to work with.

Silamide is a twisted thread that is fairly strong. It also comes in several different colors.

THREAD CONDITIONERS

Thread Heaven is an inexpensive, synthetic thread conditioner that lasts a very long time. I find that it helps to keep my thread from knotting, so I use it for all my projects.

Beeswax is a good option if you are making a vessel or a piece that needs more support. It can make your beadwork a little stiffer, but it can fill up the beads with wax. Use it sparingly so you don't clog up your beads!

There is also a **synthetic beeswax**. I like it better than natural beeswax because it doesn't fill up the beads as much and it's not as sticky.

BEADING MATS

When working with seed beads, it is always a good idea to have a soft surface to spread out your beads. I use the **vellux bead mats** that most beads stores carry.

They come in different colors and can be cleaned in the washer and dryer. Consider cutting up a vellux blanket to have lots of bead mats! **Ultra suede** or **suede** also works nicely. Glue or tape a piece of vellux or suede into a **plastic tray** (a tray without a deep side works best) for a great surface to spread out your beads. The small lip helps to keep the beads from rolling off the material.

NEEDLES

Needles come in a variety of sizes. I use **size 12 beading needles**. They are fairly long, and I find that they easily fit through seed beads with several passes of thread. They are also a little flexible, which can be an asset when you have a tight space to bead through.

A **size 11 beading needle** is slightly larger and has a larger eye. If you have a hard time threading the needle, this is a good size to use.

Some beaders like the **sharp needles**. They are much shorter than a beading needle, but they come in the same sizes as beading needles. When working with suede for bead embroidery, they can be a useful option.

TASK LAMP

Good lighting is key to beadwork. A **full-color spectrum light**, such as an OttLite, imitates natural light. This type of light is ideal for picking out colors.

Other small desk lights also work, but it's best to avoid picking out colors under a yellow-hued light; picking out the colors in sunlight will give you better results.

Some lights also come with a **magnifier**, a handy accessory for any beader.

PLIERS

It can be handy to have a small pair of pliers with smooth jaws. They can be used to break a bead to correct a mistake or to pull your thread through a bead that is getting full of thread (just be careful when you do this because you can end up breaking a bead you didn't want to break).

BEADS

Japanese seed beads come in a variety of sizes. The larger the number, the smaller the bead. The projects in this book use mostly size 11 and size 15 seed beads. Size 6 and 8 seed beads make nice accent beads. Seed beads also come in many colors and finishes. I tend to stay away from galvanized beads and those that have dyed finishes because the color can rub off or fade.

Fire polish beads are glass beads that are fairly inexpensive. They are faceted and add a nice touch to beadwork. They are measured by the millimeter.

Nothing shines quite like true **crystal beads**! I use a lot of Swarovski 4mm **bicone crystals** in these projects. **Crystal rivolis** make great focal points. (Rivolis are crystal stones, not beads, because they are not drilled.)

Glass pearls are a great combination with seed beads. Swarovski makes them in a variety of sizes and shapes. **Czech glass pearls** also look nice and can be a more affordable option.

Druk beads are round Czech glass beads. They come in a variety of sizes measured by millimeter. I like to use druk beads as clasp beads.

Delica beads, made by Miyuki of Japan, are a uniform cylinder type of bead. They are great for working peyote because they fit together nicely.

11

Basic Stitches and Techniques

Techniques are the building blocks for all beadweaving. Learn a few basic stitches and you will be on your way to creating beautiful jewelry.

WORKING WITH THREAD

The projects in this book require lots of thread, typically in varying lengths and performing multiple functions with in a piece. Here are a few definitions and guidelines to follow while creating your jewelry.

STOP BEAD

When you begin a project, you may be instructed to add a stop bead. A **stop bead** is used to prevent the beads of the project from sliding off the end of the thread. This bead may or may not be worked into the project, so it helps to read the project instructions in advance to determine its use. To add a stop bead to the thread, refer to Circle Stitch below: the thread follows the same path in one bead, without adding the extra beads.

WORKING THREAD

The **working thread** has the needle on it. When starting a new piece of thread in a piece, I like to leave about 6" (15cm) of the old thread (that now becomes a tail), then add a new thread.

To add the new thread, tie the new thread onto the thread between the beads using **half-hitch knots**. To tie a half hitch knot, go under the thread that is between the bead your working thread is coming out of and the very next bead. Leave a small loop and then go through the loop from the top with the working thread. Pull the working

thread tight and then go through the next bead. This hides the knot in between the beads. It is best to tie two or three half hitch knots between the beads when tying off your tail ends.

TAIL THREAD

The **tail thread** is the thread hanging off the piece. Tail threads can have one of two fates: they will either be used to help complete a project, or they will be left until the end of the project to be woven into the beadwork.

At the end of every project, you'll be instructed to weave in all the tail threads. To do this, thread the needle onto a tail thread. Weave this thread into the beadwork away from the place it exits from, and tie a few half-hitch knots to secure it (you do not have to weave the entire length of the thread). You can snip off any remaining old thread.

REINFORCING

The instructions will often reference "reinforcing" the work, with either the tail thread or the working thread. To reinforce, weave the working thread through the beadwork following the previous thread path. You may or may not be instructed to end the thread at this point. Reinforcing is almost always done at the clasp ends of bracelets and necklaces.

CIRCLE STITCH

A circle stitch looks just like it sounds: The thread path makes a circle. Circle stitching is used a lot in the projects because it's a great way to bring various elements together.

CIRCLE STITCH

The working thread will come out of a bead and then, whether or not it goes through one or more beads, the thread always makes a circle and goes back through the bead it originally exited from on the opposite side.

PICOT STITCHES

Picot stitches are usually used as an edging detail, but they can also be incorporated into a design. As with most stitches, there are several variations.

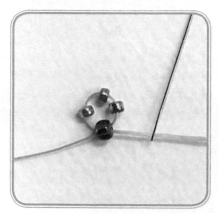

CIRCULAR PICOT STITCH

In general, the working thread should come out of a bead. Pick up three beads and go back through the bead that the working thread exited from on the opposite side, forming a beaded loop. This makes a circular picot stitch.

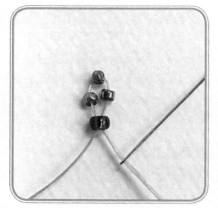

TRIANGULAR PICOT STITCH

In general, the working thread should be coming out of a bead. Pick up three beads and go back through the bead the working thread originally exited from on the same side. This creates a more triangular picot.

NETTING BASICS

Netting creates a more open style of beadwork, giving it a lacy feel. There are many variations of netting but a few basic rules apply to it. An odd number of beads is usually used to create the nets so there is a center bead to pass through. Netting can be done as a tube, as in the chain for the *Reversible Pendant Lariat* (page 58), or it can be done flat, as in the *Dewdrop Flower Bracelet* (page 29). There are other variations as well.

NETTED PIECE

The netted piece begins with a loop of beads. More beads are added to help create the arches, or nets, around the original bead loop. The nets on each row are increased by two beads for each row.

This photo shows a flat, round piece of netting. I use this in several of the designs, such as the Dewdrop Flower Bracelet *(page 29) and the* Victorian Cabochon Necklace *(page 48). It makes a great component that can be used as a base for a crystal bezel or as a design element on its own.*

tip

For most of the designs in this book, I use a solid color of beads for the netting. However, if you are having a hard time understanding the netting process, use an accent bead as the middle bead for practice. For example, if the pattern calls for five beads, the middle bead will be the third bead, so use an accent bead for the third bead.

FRINGE BASICS

Fringe is one of my favorite parts of beadwork; I love the way it swings and creates movement. Fringe can be long, short, full or anywhere in between. Seed beads make for better fringe; the rounded edges of the seed beads make them lay smoother than the straight edges of delica beads. Adding a few large beads to the fringe will create weight, and the fringe will usually hang better. As with so much beadwork, there are endless variations of fringe; here, I show you my two favorite types and the ones used most often in the following projects.

STRAIGHT FRINGE

A straight fringe is the most common type of fringe and has many uses. I often use three seed beads after my last fringe bead to create a picot (see Triangular Picot Stitch on page 12) under the bead. Other options include using one seed bead or even four seed beads. (If you use four seed beads, go back up the first seed bead you picked and then go up through the other fringe beads; this creates a little diamond under the last bead.)

LOOPED FRINGE

Looped fringe is another option. You make large circular picot stitches (see Circular Picot Stitch on page 12) but you add more beads. Bead counts should be the same on both sides of the circle to ensure the fringe hangs evenly.

tip

Pinch the last beads of the fringe between your fingernails after you have gone back up the fringe with your working thread. This creates just a tiny space so that the fringe isn't so tight.

FLAT BRICK STITCH

Flat brick stitch usually makes for a sturdy piece of beadwork. Flat brick stitch always has a base row; I find it easier to do decreases rather than increases when working flat brick stitch, so I always start with the longest row as my base row. After the base row, the remaining rows are worked by adding beads and going under the existing threads from the rows and then going back up the beads.

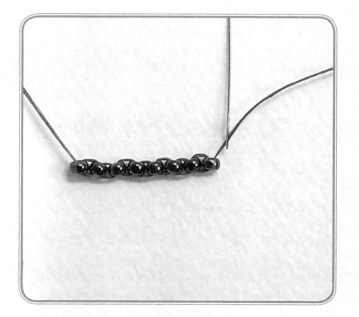

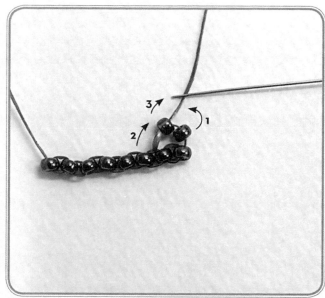

1. Base row

Begin the base row by picking up two beads and going back through them from the tail end. They should sit side by side. Pick up one more bead and go back through the last bead added on the opposite side from where the thread originally exited and also go through the bead you just picked up. This makes the new bead sit next to the other beads. Keep adding beads this way until the row is the desired length.

2. Begin row two

Pick up two beads and go under the second thread from the back to the front and go up the second bead (1). Then go down the first bead and come back up the second bead (2–3). This makes the first two beads sit closer together.

3. Continue pattern

Pick up one bead and go under the next thread from the back to the front and go back up the bead just added. Keep adding beads this way until you have one less bead in this row than the base row. Repeat steps 2–3 until the beadwork is the desired size.

TUBULAR BRICK STITCH

Just like flat brick stitch, tubular brick stitch makes for a sturdy piece of beadwork. It is also a good rope to use for pendants. Tubular brick stitch, especially when done with only a few beads, can be tricky to get started, but it is well worth the effort. The finished rope is strong and appears to be twisted.

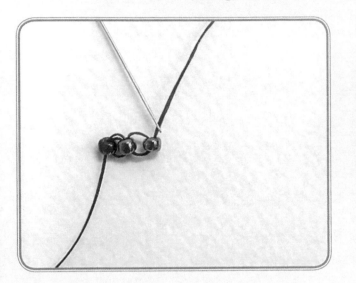

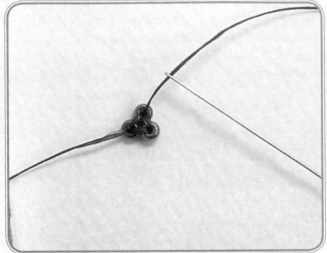

1. Begin first row

Start by picking up two beads. Then go back through them from the tail end. This will make them sit side by side.

Pick up one bead and go through the bead the thread is exiting from on the opposite side and also go through the bead just picked up.

2. Form triangle

Circle stitch the first bead to the last bead. This will make a small triangle. The working thread should be coming out of the top of one of the beads.

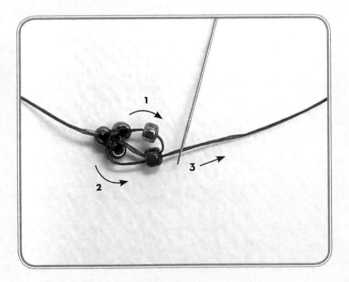

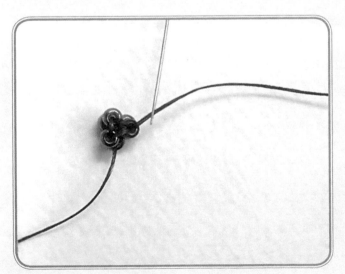

3. Begin second row

Pick up two beads and go under the second thread from where the thread is exiting (1). Go back up the second bead (2–3). This will make the two beads sit on top of the original three beads.

4. Continue pattern

Pick up one bead and go under the next thread. Then go back up the bead that was just picked up. Also go down through the first bead of this row and come up the next bead. This adds the last thread that connects the triangle together. Three beads should now be connected by three threads.

Repeat steps 3–4 until the rope is the desired length.

FLAT PEYOTE

Flat peyote is a very versatile stitch. I use it to make flower petals as in the *Flower Garden Necklace* (page 86). The basic concept of peyote is that you start with a base row of beads and add more rows from there. If you are new to peyote stitch, it is always easier to use an even number of beads. Odd count peyote has its uses, but it requires a different turnaround at the end of each row.

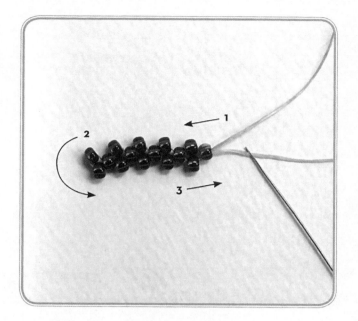

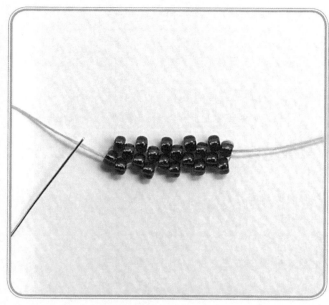

1. Base row

Pick up beads until you reach the desired width (in this case, I picked up ten beads). After the base row of beads is picked up, pick up another bead, skip the last bead of the original row and go through the next bead. Continue adding beads this way until you get to the end of the row.

Notice that the rows look like little bricks or a zipper. The beads that stick up are often referred to as "up" beads, and the recessed beads are referred to as "down" beads.

2. Add another row

For the next row, the beads that are added will fit into the recessed spaces. Pick up one bead and go through the last bead that sticks up from the last row. Keep repeating down the row. Keep adding rows this way until the beadwork is the desired length.

tip

The base row is usually considered rows 1 and 2 because all subsequent rows will only need half the number of beads to complete the row.

DIAGONAL PEYOTE

Diagonal peyote is a variation of flat peyote that makes a nice strap. I use this stitch in the *Lacy Flower Necklace* (page 130), but small pieces can also be used for leaves or flowers.

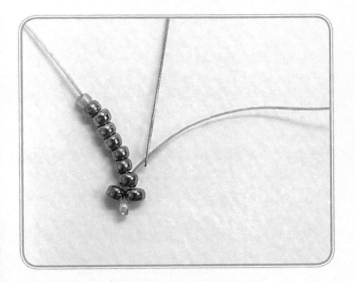

1. Begin first row

To start diagonal peyote, pick up one accent bead and turn it into a stop bead by going back through it from the tail end. Then pick up eight main beads, an accent bead and another main bead. Go back through the seventh main bead. This will create a triangular picot with the accent bead at the tip (see *Picot Stitches* on page 12).

2. Add second row

Pick up one main bead, skip the next bead and go through the next one. Repeat two more times. The thread should now be coming out of the first main bead of the first row.

3. Turn corner

Pick up two accent beads and go down through the main bead that is sticking out. This positions the needle and thread to go back down the beadwork.

4. Add third row

Pick up one main color bead and go through the next bead that is sticking out. Repeat two more times. This should bring the thread out of the bottom main bead.

5. Turn corner

Pick up two main beads, one accent and one more main bead. Then go up through the first main bead that was picked up to create a triangular picot. Pull this snug against the other beads.

6. Add next row

Pick up one main bead and go up through the bead that is sticking out. Repeat two more times.

7. Turn corner

Pick up three accent beads and go back down the main bead that is sticking out (it is the last main bead added).

8. Continue pattern

Pick up one main bead and go through the next bead that is sticking out. Repeat two more times. The thread should now be coming out of the bottom main bead. Repeat steps 5–8 until the beadwork is the desired length.

ADHESIVE BASICS FOR BEAD EMBROIDERY

When starting a piece of bead embroidery, there is often a focal cabochon or crystal that needs to be adhered to a work surface before you can start. I like to use medium to heavy interfacing as my work surface. Always be sure to leave plenty of extra interfacing around the edges of your cabochon or crystal. You can always trim extra interfacing off, but it is much harder to add if you don't start with a big enough piece.

For the most part, I like to use a glue like E6000 to put my crystals and cabochons in place. Another option is to use double-sided tacky tape; if you are using vintage crystals, this is the preferred method. The foiling on the back of vintage crystals can come off with the glue, so use the tape instead.

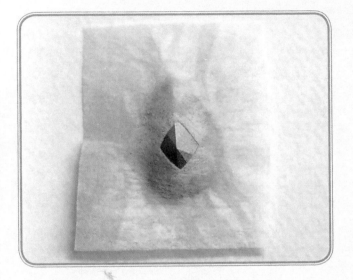

This shows the back of a pointed crystal with interfacing. The interfacing has a diamond shape cut into the middle to allow for the pointed back of the crystal.

Adhere crystal or cabochon

If you have a slightly pointed crystal, fold the piece of interfacing in half and then in half again. Snip a small piece off the folded corner to make a small diamond-shaped hole in the center of the interfacing. Then when you glue or tape the crystal to the interfacing, the point can go through the small hole you created.

To glue the crystal or cabochon: Use a toothpick to spread a thin layer of glue onto the back of the crystal or cabochon. It doesn't take much. Then press the piece onto the interfacing. If any glue seeps out around the edges, wipe if off. (It is really hard to sew through the glue, so be sure to do this.) It doesn't take long for the glue to set enough for you to start beading.

To tape the crystal or cabochon: Cut small pieces of the tape and place them around the crystal as close to the edges as possible. (Don't use good scissors to cut the tape; it is very hard on scissors! Don't let the tape stick out from under the crystal; it is just as hard to sew through as the glue.)

After you have your crystal or cabochon in place, you are ready to start beading. When you start working, you can always go back and add a dab of glue or a little piece of tape if an area isn't sticking enough.

BACKSTITCH FOR BEAD EMBROIDERY

Bead embroidery can be worked on any number of surfaces. The backstitch is used to sew beads onto the work surface. It is a good basic stitch for embellishing or for creating the base row to build a peyote bezel. A bezel is a beautiful way to incorporate a loose crystal or cabochon into a design by enclosing the edge tightly with beads. I like to use a medium to heavy interfacing (the kind without the iron-on fusing) as my work surface.

When sewing around a crystal or cabochon, work in the direction that feels most comfortable for you.

Begin bead embroidery

Adhere the crystal or cabochon to the interfacing (see *Adhesive Basics for Bead Embroidery* on page 20).

Start a new thread and put a knot at the end that is large enough to hold in the interfacing. Beginning on the longer side of the crystal or cabochon rather than at a curve or point, bring the needle and thread up through the interfacing to the top side. It helps if you work at a slight angle so the stitches stay as close to the crystal as possible.

Pick up three beads, pull them down the thread and lay them alongside the crystal or cabochon. Sew down at the end of them. Come back up the interfacing at the beginning of the beads (where the knot is) and sew through all three beads again.

Pick up three beads, pull them down the thread to lay them along the crystal in line with the first three beads and sew down at the end of them. Come back up between the beads and the crystal and go through the last bead in the previous group and the three beads just added. You are going through four beads at this point. (This connects the three beads just added with the previous three beads and results in the beads laying more evenly around the crystal.)

Continue working backstitch around the rest of the crystal or cabochon.

When you are finished stitching, bring the thread to the back of the piece. Tie the thread to secure it, and trim off any excess thread.

Backstitch for bead embroidery pattern

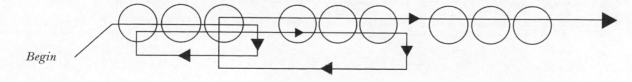

Begin

Projects

Beaded jewelry has a fabulous trait:
It can easily fit each individual person.
There are no size limitations because
bracelets and necklaces can easily be made
smaller or larger. Beads come in so many
different and beautiful colors, and that makes
it easy to make something to go with every
mood, every outfit and every occasion.

The projects here cover a range of romantic styles.
Are you feeling bold? Try the *Netted Collar* (page 24)
or the *Scalloped Lace Necklace* (page 70). If you're in a
coquettish state of mind, perhaps the *Chain Lariat*
(page 112) or the *Pearl and Crystal Bracelet* (page 64)
will suit you. The *Flower Garden Necklace* (page 86) will
add glamour to a garden party, while the *Pearl Daisy
Bracelet* (page 76) can dress up jeans and a T-shirt.

After you have mastered a project, experiment with
different bead sizes and even shapes. Just by making small
changes, a piece can look completely different. Play with
the bead size of the *Crystal Bracelet* (page 42) for more
width or the *Wavy Rosette Necklace* (page 115) for more
dramatic twists and turns. Different color schemes can
even change the look and feel of a piece; try smoky, dark
beads for the *Tiara Necklace* (page 118) to take the piece
from elegant to outgoing.

The rating system is just a guideline to help the more
inexperienced beader decide where to start. It's not a hard
and fast rule. One-star projects are suitable for beginners to
advanced beaders. These are good projects to start with.
No previous beadweaving knowledge is necessary. Two-
star projects are suitable for intermediate to advanced
beaders. It helps to have a little beadweaving experience
under your belt before you try these projects. Three-star
projects are suitable for advanced beaders. Don't start with
these projects unless you are familiar with the stitches or
techniques used or have some beadweaving experience. It
is always a good idea to read through all the instructions
before starting a project. This often helps with understanding the directions better after you actually start the project.

NETTED COLLAR

This necklace is a great alternative for women who don't necessarily like chokers but like the look of them. The collar drapes nicely around the neck and has an adjustable clasp, making it an ideal choice for a fit that's close, but not too close.

Materials

size 12 beading needle

size D Nymo thread

ten 4mm bicone crystals

eight drop beads

four 3mm beads

one 6mm bead

26 grams size 11 Japanese seed beads for main color

2 grams size 15 Japanese seed beads for accent color

TWO STARS

Collar pattern 1

Thread the beading needle onto 2yd. (2m) of thread, single thickness with no knot. Pick up one main color bead and turn it into a stopper bead by going back through it from the tail end. Leave a 10"-12" (25cm-30cm) tail. (This bead is incorporated into the design.)

Pick up 15 main color beads for a total of 16 beads. Go back through the seventh bead of the 16 beads, working toward the tail end.

Collar pattern 2

Pick up five main color beads and go through the bead that your tail is coming out of.

Collar pattern 3

Pick up six main color beads and go back down the third bead of the five beads from the previous group.

tip

If you have a hard time telling which are the five beads you added previously, pull the last stitch a little loose so you can see the beads. You can always pull the stitch tight again after you go through the third bead.

Collar pattern 4

Pick up five main color beads and go down through the third bead below the connection that was made earlier (the sixth bead from where your thread is exiting).

Collar pattern 5

Pick up six main color beads and go back up through the third bead of the five beads added previously.

Collar pattern 6

Pick up five beads and go through the third bead after the previous connection (the sixth bead from where the thread is exiting).

Collar pattern 7

Pick up six main color beads and go back down through the third bead of the five beads added in collar pattern 6.

Collar pattern 8

Pick up five main color beads and go down through the third bead after the connection (the sixth bead from where the thread is exiting).

Collar pattern 9

Pick up six main color beads and go back up the third bead of the five beads added previously.

Collar pattern 10

Pick up five main color beads and go back up through the third bead above the connection (the sixth bead from where the thread is exiting). If done correctly, the top and bottom edges of the netting will have three beads between each net. Repeat collar patterns 7-10 until the netting is the desired length (see the tip below).

tip

For most people, 18" (46cm) is a good approximate length. The top edge of the netting will be slightly gathered, and this will shorten the necklace. The clasp is also adjustable.

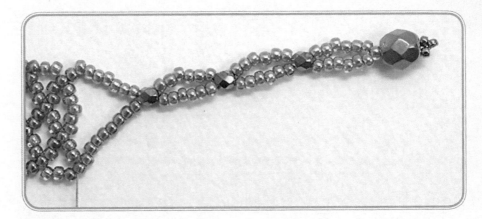

Collar clasp 1

Weave the working thread so it is coming out of the end bead of the netting.

Pick up eight main color beads, one 3mm bead, six main color beads, one 3mm bead, six main color beads, one 3mm bead, seven main color beads, the 6mm bead and then three accent beads. Skip the three accent beads and go back through the 6mm bead and the next main color bead.

Pick up six main color beads and go back through the next 3mm bead. Repeat two more times. Then pick up eight main color beads and go through the end bead on the other side of the netting. Reinforce.

Embellish border 1

Start a new thread approximately 2yd. (2m) long, single thickness with no knot. Weave it so it is coming out of the middle bead (the second bead) of the first group of three beads on the edge of the netting. Pick up three accent beads and go through the next middle bead (second bead) of the next group of three beads on the side of the netting.

Embellish border 2

Pick up two accent beads and go through the next middle bead of the next group of three beads on the side of the netting.

Repeat embellish border 1-2 until you reach the end of the netting. Then pull the thread snug. This will make the netting gently curve on one side. Weave in and tie off the working thread.

Collar clasp 2

Weave the tail thread you left earlier and come out of the end bead of the netting. Pick up eight main color beads, one 3mm bead and eight main color beads. Go through the netting on the opposite side from where the thread originally exited. Weave through the end beads of the netting and go back through the first eight beads and the 3mm bead.

Collar clasp 3

Pick up thirteen main color beads and go back through the 3mm bead on the opposite side from where the thread originally exited and also go through the first seven main color beads to make a circle. Repeat this step for four more circles using thirteen main color beads. Reinforce.

Circular fringe pattern 1

Start a new thread approximately 2yd. (2m) long, single thickness with no knot. Fold the collar in half and find the group of three beads at the bottom edge of the netting (the side without the gather) that are closest to the center of the collar.

Use a spare needle to mark the middle bead of the group of three center beads. Count over from the center beads to the eighth three bead group (don't count the center beads as one of the eight). Weave the working thread in so it is coming out of the middle bead of the eighth group from the center going toward the center of the necklace.

Pick up three main color beads, one accent bead, one 4mm crystal, one accent bead, six main color beads, one drop bead and then six more main color beads. Go back through the accent bead, the crystal and the next accent bead so they form a circle.

Circular fringe pattern 2

Pick up three main color beads, skip over the next group of three beads and go through the middle bead of the next group of three beads.

Circular fringe pattern 3

Pick up ten main color beads, one accent bead, one 4mm crystal, one accent bead, six main color beads, one drop bead and six main color beads. Go back through the accent beads and the crystal so they form a circle.

Pick up ten main color beads, skip over the next three groups of three beads and go through the middle bead of the fourth group.

Circular fringe pattern 4

Repeat fringe pattern 3 two more times and then repeat the first fringe you made. There are five fringes on the first layer of fringe.

Circular fringe pattern 5

Weave your thread so it is coming out of the third group of three beads counting over from the center group, working toward the center of the collar.

Pick up ten main color beads, one accent bead, one 4mm crystal, one accent bead, six main color beads, one accent bead, one 4mm crystal, one accent bead, six main color beads, one drop bead and then six main color beads. Go back through the last set of accent beads and the crystal to form a circle.

Circular fringe pattern 6

Pick up six main color beads and go through the next set of accent beads and crystal to form another circle. Pick up ten main color beads, skip two groups of three beads and go through the middle bead of the center group of beads.

Repeat fringe patterns 5–6 one more time. There are two fringes on the second layer of fringe.

Circular fringe pattern 7

Weave the working thread so it is coming out of the second group of three beads left of the center, with the thread going toward the center of the collar.

Pick up twenty-eight main color beads, one accent bead, one 4mm crystal, one accent bead, six main color beads, one drop bead and six more main color beads. Go back through the accent beads and the crystal so they form a circle.

Pick up twenty-eight main color beads and go through the second group of three beads on the other side of the center group. The third and final layer of fringe has one fringe. Tie off any remaining threads.

DEWDROP FLOWER BRACELET

The centerpiece of this bracelet is a whimsical flower featuring a ruffled-netting bezel that frames a crystal. Because crystal rivolis have no holes, you have to create a bezel to hold them. This bracelet fits best if it is made to fit snugly around the wrist.

Materials

size 12 beading needle

size D Nymo thread

forty-five tiny drop beads

one 8mm round bead

one 14mm rivoli crystal

3 grams size 15 Japanese seed beads for the flower

7 grams size 15 Japanese seed beads for the band

3 grams size 11 Japanese seed beads for the leaves

TWO STARS

Bezel pattern 1

Start with 2yd. (2m) of thread, single thickness with no knot. Pick up twelve flower beads and go back through all of them from the tail end. Leave a 4"–6" (10cm–15cm) tail. Go through one more bead (this will make the circle more uniform). Pick up three flower beads, skip over one bead and go through the next bead of the original circle.

Bezel pattern 2

Repeat until there are six points. On the sixth point, also go through the first two beads of the first point created in this row. This lines the thread up for the next row.

Bezel pattern 3

Pick up five flower beads and go through the middle bead (the second bead) of the next point. Repeat until there are six new points with five beads. On the sixth point, also go through the first three beads of the first point of this row.

Bezel pattern 4

Pick up seven flower beads and go through the middle bead (the third bead) of the next point. Repeat until there are six new points with seven beads. On the sixth point, also go through the first four beads of the first point of this row.

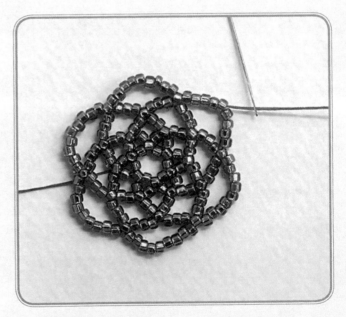

Bezel pattern 5

Pick up nine flower beads and go through the middle bead (the fourth bead) of the next point. Repeat until you have added six points with nine beads. On the sixth point, also go through the first five beads of the first point of this row.

Bezel pattern 6

Pick up five flower beads and go through the middle bead (the fifth bead) of the next point. This row decreases, so it will begin to pull the netting in. Repeat until there are six points.

After completing the sixth point, place the crystal into the center of the netting. Pull the thread snug so the netting firmly encloses the crystal.

Go through the first three beads of the first point of this row.

Bezel pattern 7

Pick up three flower beads, skip two beads and go through the next bead (the bead you go through is actually the middle bead from a point of the row with nine beads). Pick up three more beads and go through the middle bead of the last row with five beads. Repeat this around the last row of netting.

There should now be twelve points. The netting is increased. This row should stand up from the last row. Go through the first two beads of this row.

Bezel pattern 8

Pick up one flower bead, one tiny drop bead and one more flower bead. Go through the middle bead (the second bead) of the next point. Repeat until there are twelve points with a tiny drop bead.

When this row is done, do not needle up to the middle bead of the first point of this row; go through the one bead that is the point of the previous row.

Bezel pattern 9

The working thread should now be coming out of the point bead from the previous row. This next row of points sits behind the row just created. The points will be created by going through the same beads used to create the last row with the tiny drops.

Pick up five flower beads and go through the next middle point bead of the previous row. Make sure this new point sits behind the tiny drop.

Repeat until there are twelve points. For this row, go through the first three beads of the first point of this row. This photo shows the back side of the crystal.

Bezel pattern 10

Pick up three flower beads, one tiny drop bead and three more flower beads. Go through the middle bead (the third bead) of the next point. Repeat until there are twelve points with the tiny drop beads.

This completes the flower. Tie off the tail thread and the working thread. Set the flower aside for now.

31

Chain pattern 1

Start a new thread, approximately 2yd. (2m), single thickness with no knot. Pick up one band bead and turn it into a stopper bead by going back through it from the tail end. Leave a 10"-12" (25cm-30cm) tail.

Pick up twelve more band beads, for a total of thirteen beads. Skip the last (thirteenth) bead and go back through the next (twelfth) bead, working toward the tail end.

Chain pattern 2

Pick up three band beads, skip the next three beads and go through the fourth bead.

Chain pattern 3

Pick up three band beads, skip the next three beads and go through the fourth bead.

Chain pattern 4

Pick up three band beads. Skip the last bead that was just picked up and go through the second bead.

Chain pattern 5

Pick up three more band beads and go through the middle bead of the group of three beads that is below the connection (it is the fourth bead away from where the thread is exiting).

Chain pattern 6

Pick up three band beads and go through the middle bead of the next group of three beads below the next connection (it is the fourth bead away from where the thread is exiting).

Repeat chain pattern 4–6 until the band is the desired length. A good sample length is 2½" (6cm) for each side. The clasp bead and loop take up about 1" (3cm) so remember to allow for that.

When you finish one band, repeat chain pattern 1–6 to make another band the same length. Count the beads that stick out on the edges of the bands to get the bands exactly the same length.

Assembly 1

Put a needle on the tail thread from the band and weave it so it is coming out of third bead at the end. Go through the middle point bead (the fourth bead) of the fourth row of netting on the back of the flower. (It is the row with seven beads for the points.)

Weave over to the next seven-bead point and come out of the fourth bead. Go through the third bead on the other end of the band. Reinforce this several times.

Assembly 2

Repeat the instructions in assembly 1 for the other side of the flower with the second band piece.

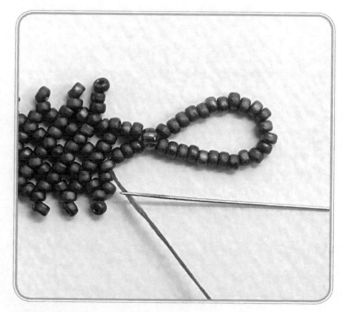

Assembly 3

Put a needle back on the working thread at the end of the band. If you didn't end the band with three beads on the edge, do that now. Then weave the working thread so it is coming out of the fifth bead from the end.

Pick up four band beads, the 8mm bead and three more band beads. Skip the three band beads and go back through the 8mm bead and the next band bead. Pick up three band beads and go through the fifth bead on the band, counting from the other side of the band. Reinforce.

Assembly 4

Put a needle on the working thread on the other band. Weave the thread so it is coming out of the fifth bead from the end.

Pick up three band beads, one leaf bead and then enough band beads to fit comfortably but snugly around the clasp bead. Go back through the leaf bead and pick up three more band beads. Go through the fifth bead from the end on the other side of the band. Reinforce.

33

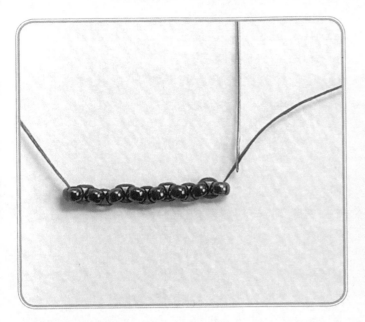

Leaves pattern 1

The leaves are worked in the flat brick stitch (see *Flat Brick Stitch* on page 15) in the following pattern.

Start a new thread, approximately 1½yd. (1.5m), single thickness with no knot. Pick up two leaf beads and go back through them from the tail end. They should sit side by side. Leave a 4"–6" (10cm–15cm) tail.

Pick up one more leaf bead. Go back through the last bead added on the opposite side from where the thread originally exited and also go through the bead just picked up. This will make the new bead sit next to the other beads. Keep adding beads until there are a total of eight leaf beads.

Leaves pattern 2

Pick up two leaf beads. Go under the second thread from the back to the front and go up the second leaf bead (1). Go down the first leaf bead and come back up the second leaf bead (2–3). This will make them sit closer together.

Leaves pattern 3

Pick up one more leaf bead and go under the next thread from the back to the front and go back up the bead just added. Keep adding beads this way until you have a total of seven beads in this row.

Leaves pattern 4

Keep working rows following leaves pattern 2–3 until you get down to a row of two beads. (Each row will decrease by one bead.)

Leaves pattern 5

Now weave the working thread down the side of the triangle and come out of an end bead on the row of eight beads. Continue making rows on this side of the triangle following leaves pattern 2–4.

For the end of the leaf that goes down to one bead after the row of two beads, the working thread should be coming out of one of the two beads. Pick up one leaf bead and go down the bead next to it. This will make the last bead sit on top of the two-bead row. The leaf is now a diamond shape.

Leaves pattern 6

Put the needle on the tail thread and run it through all the outside edge beads and pull it snug. This will make the leaf curl slightly. Weave in the tail thread.

Make another leaf following leaves pattern 1–6. There are two on the bracelet.

Assembly 5

Weave the working thread (you need approximately 8"–10" [20cm–25cm] of thread) on the leaf and come out of one of the two beads at the end of it.

Go through the middle (fifth bead) of the nine-bead point above the band connection to the flower. The leaf sits between the flower and the band. Go through the bead of the leaf next to the one the thread originally exited from. (The band is folded back in the photo to show the connection.) Reinforce.

Repeat on the other side of the flower with the other leaf.

Branch fringe embellishment

Weave the working thread (you need approximately 18" [46cm] of thread) so it is coming out of the middle (fifth bead) of the nine bead point where the leaf is connected. (If this bead is too full of thread, weave over to a bead of the flower that is close to it.)

Pick up sixteen to twenty band beads, one leaf bead and one tiny drop bead. Skip the tiny drop bead and go back through the leaf bead and several of the band beads. This is the main stem of the branch fringe.

Pick up a few more band beads, one leaf bead and another tiny drop bead. Skip the drop bead and go back through the leaf bead and the band beads just added and a few more of the band beads of the original stem. This creates a branch off the original stem.

Make another branch or two off this fringe and then make one more branch fringe on this side of the flower.

Make two branch fringes on the other side of the flower. The bead count can vary because the fringes do not have to be symmetrical. It is more of a free-form fringe. Tie off any remaining threads.

COSMIC CRYSTAL NECKLACE

This was one of my earliest designs that used a crystal rivoli. When I first saw the rivolis, I knew I wanted to use them in my jewelry. Because crystal rivolis have no holes, you have to create a bezel to hold them. This design uses a netting technique for the bezel, and that element is carried throughout the necklace.

Materials

size 12 beading needle

size D Nymo thread

one 18mm rivoli crystal

six 4mm bicone crystals

two 8mm round crystals

one drop bead

one 8mm fire polish bead

6 grams size 15 Japanese seed beads for main color

3 grams size 15 Japanese seed beads for accent color

✦ **ONE STAR**

Focal bezel pattern 1

Start with approximately 2yd. (2m) of thread, single thickness with no knot. Pick up thirty main color beads and go back through them from the tail end. Go through a few more beads to close the circle tighter.

Focal bezel pattern 2

Pick up seven main color beads. Count over five beads, but do not count the bead the thread is coming out of. Go through the fifth bead. Repeat this five more times. There should be a total of six points or triangles around the circle.

Focal bezel pattern 3

After the last triangle is added, go through the first four beads of the first triangle. This lines you up to start the next row.

Focal bezel pattern 4

Pick up thirteen main color beads and go through the point of the next triangle from the last row (it will be the fourth bead).

Repeat five more times for a total of six points.

Focal bezel pattern 5

After the sixth triangle is added, needle up to the point of the first triangle of this row, which would be the seventh bead.

Focal bezel pattern 6

For the last row of the bezel, pick up seven main color beads and go through the point of the triangle from the previous row (the seventh bead). This row will make the bezel start to curl up, which is necessary to hold the crystal rivoli in place. Repeat the seven bead triangles until you get to the last one.

Before you complete the last triangle, insert the crystal rivoli inside the netting. Make the last point of this row and be sure to pull it snug.

Weave back through the beads of the last row to reinforce and to help secure the crystal rivoli in place. Tie off the tail thread and leave the working thread. It will be used later.

Accent pattern 1

Start a new thread, approximately 1yd. (1m), single thickness with no knot.

Pick up fifteen main color beads and go back through them from the tail end to create a circle. Go through a few more beads to close the circle tighter.

Pick up five main color beads and count over three beads. Go through the third bead.

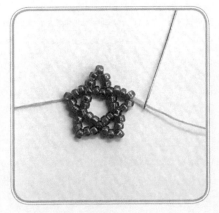

Accent pattern 2

Repeat four more times for a total of five points. This makes a small star.

Make seven more stars following accent pattern 1–2. Also make one small star in the accent color.

Accent pattern 3

The eight small stars of the main color are embellished (do not embellish the accent color star). To do this, weave the working thread down to the original circle of fifteen beads and come out of the bead that is shared with the first row of triangles.

Accent pattern 4

Pick up three accent beads and go through the next bead of the original circle that is shared by the row of triangles. (You are skipping over two beads.) This creates a picot (see *Picot Stitches* on page 12).

Accent pattern 5

Repeat four more times. There should be a total of five picots that stand up from the star.

Repeat accent pattern 3–5 on the remaining seven main color stars.

Accent pattern 6

Next you will add a 4mm crystal to two of the main color stars and also to the accent color star.

The working thread should be coming out of a bead of the original circle. Pick up one of the 4mm crystals and go back through a bead of the original circle on the other side from where the thread originally exited. This will make the crystal lay in the center of the star. Reinforce.

Repeat this step on one more main color star and also on the accent color star. Tie off the tail and working threads on all the stars.

Accent pattern 7

Start a new thread, approximately 1½yd. (1.5m), single thickness with no knot. Make another main color star following accent pattern 1–2. When you finish this, add another row of points to make it into a large star.

The working thread should be coming out of the point bead of the last row (third bead). Pick up seven beads and go through the point bead of the next triangle. Repeat four more times.

Tie off the tail thread but leave the working thread.

Accent pattern 8

Attach the small accent color star to the large main color star using the working thread from the large star. There is no right or wrong thread path to attach the stars together.

Center the small star on the large star and go through several beads on both stars to tack them together.

Accent pattern 9

Pick up the large star and weave the working thread so it is coming out of a point bead of one of the triangles.

Pick up three main color beads, one accent bead, one 4mm crystal, one accent bead, six main color beads, one drop bead and four more accent beads. Skip the last three accent beads and go back up the next accent bead, the drop bead and the next main color bead.

Then pick up four main color beads and go through the next main color bead, the accent bead, the 4mm crystal and the next accent bead.

Pick up three more main color beads and go through the point bead the thread originally exited from on the opposite side.

Assembly 1

To attach the double star to the crystal bezel, weave the working thread so it is coming out of the point bead of the third triangle up from where the fringe is attached.

Pick up one main color bead, one of the 4mm crystals and one main color bead. Go through the fourth bead on the second-to-last row of the bezel around the crystal and go back down the beads you just picked up.

Go through the point bead the thread originally exited from on the opposite side.

Assembly 2

Weave over to the point bead of the next triangle and pick up one main color bead, one 4mm crystal and one main color bead. Skip over the next point of the bezel and go through the fourth bead on the second-to-last row of the bezel of the next point. Go back through the beads you just picked up.

Go through the point bead the thread originally exited from on the opposite side.

Weave in and tie off the working thread.

Assembly 3

Weave the working thread from the bezel up to the triangle that is to the side of the center top triangle. Come out of the fourth bead.

Attach a small star with a 4mm crystal with a circle stitch (see *Circle Stitch* on page 13) at one of the points of the star's triangle.

Assembly 4

Weave over and attach the point bead of the star's next triangle to the fourth bead of the bezel.

Assembly 5

Weave the working thread up to the point of the star's top triangle. Using the circle stitch, attach another star (one without a crystal) at the points of the triangles.

Assembly 6

To add the next part of the strap, weave the working thread so it is coming out of the third point of the star.

Pick up three main color beads, one of the 8mm crystals and three main color beads. Go through the point of another small star.

Assembly 7

Weave over to the next point of the star. Pick up three main color beads and go back through the 8mm crystal.

Pick up three more main color beads and go through the point on the right-hand side of the next star.

Assembly 8

Weave back up to the last star that was added and come out of the top point of the triangle. Then circle stitch another star to the star the working thread is coming out of.

Assembly 9

Weave up to the third point and come out of the far side of the bead. Then pick up eight main color beads, one accent bead and eight more main color beads. Go through the next point of the next triangle, weave through the star and back up the first eight main color beads and come out of the accent bead.

Pick up eight main color beads, one accent bead and eight main color beads. Go back through the accent bead the thread is exiting from on the opposite side. Go back through the first eight beads you picked up and the accent bead. Repeat this until the strap is the desired length.

To add the 8mm fire polish bead for the clasp, pick up eight main color beads, the 8mm fire polish bead and three accent beads. Skip the accent beads and go back through the 8mm fire polish bead. Pick up eight main color beads and go back through the accent bead your thread originally exited from on the opposite side. Reinforce.

Repeat assembly pattern 3–8 for the other side of the necklace. Create a loop of main color beads that fits comfortably but snugly around the 8mm fire polish bead. Tie off any remaining threads.

CRYSTAL BRACELET

Crystals are one of my favorite types of beads to work with. Their sparkle just makes me smile. Judging by the popularity of crystal jewelry, I am not the only one who feels this way. This is my version of the classic tennis bracelet, only wider and with more sparkle. It looks great with jeans or with a special dress.

Materials

size 12 beading needle

size D Nymo or Fireline beading thread

ninety-three 4mm bicone crystals

one 8mm fire polish bead

6 grams size 11 Japanese seed beads for main color

3 grams size 15 Japanese seed beads for accent color

ONE STAR

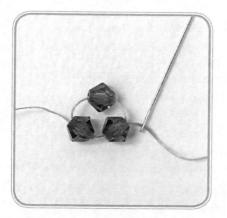

Bracelet strap pattern 1

Start with approximately 2½yd. (2.5m) of thread, single thickness with no knot. Pick up three crystals and go back through the first two crystals from the tail end. Leave a 10"–12" (25cm–30cm) tail. This will be used later for the loop part of the clasp. Pull snug.

Bracelet strap pattern 2

Pick up two more crystals and go back through the crystal that the thread exited from on the opposite side. Also, go through the first crystal of the two crystals that were just added. Pull snug.

Keep adding crystals in this way until the bracelet is the desired length. A good average length is approximately 6½" (17cm).

Bracelet strap pattern 3

Weave the working thread so it is coming out of the first crystal on the side of the bracelet.

Embellishment pattern 1

Pick up one size 15 bead, one size 11 bead and then three size 15 beads. Go back through the size 11 bead on the opposite side from where the thread originally exited. This creates a picot out of the three size 15 beads that will sit on top of the size 11 bead.

Embellishment pattern 2

Pick up one more size 15 bead and go through the next crystal on the side of the bracelet.

Repeat embellishment pattern 1–2, making picots between the crystals. At the end of the first side of the bracelet, weave the working thread through the end bead and then continue making picots on the other side of the bracelet.

Embellishment pattern 3

Weave the working thread so it is coming out of the tip bead (the center bead) of the first picot you created.

Embellishment pattern 4

Pick up one size 15 bead and then five size 11 beads. Go back through the second size 11 bead you picked up on the opposite side from where the thread originally exited. This will make a picot out of the last four size 11 beads.

Embellishment pattern 5

Pick up one size 11 bead and one size 15 bead and go through the tip bead of the next picot from the previous row.

Keep making picots following embellishment pattern 4-5 until you have gone down the side of the bracelet. At the end of the bracelet, weave the working thread through the end beads and continue making picots on the other side of the bracelet.

Bracelet closure 1

Weave the working thread so it is coming out of the end crystal.

Pick up five size 11 beads, the 8mm fire polish bead and three size 11 beads. Skip the last three size 11 beads and go back through the 8mm bead and the next size 11 bead.

Pick up four or five more size 11 beads and go back through the crystal on the opposite side from where the thread originally exited. (The number of beads you need to pick up may vary slightly because the end crystal is at a slight angle and the clasp bead may sit more evenly if you add an extra bead.) Reinforce.

Bracelet closure 2

Put a needle on the tail thread and weave it so it is coming out of the end crystal.

Pick up five size 11 beads and then enough size 11 beads to go comfortably but snugly around the 8mm bead. Go back through the fifth size 11 bead you picked up.

Pick up four or five more main color beads and go back through the crystal on the opposite side from where the thread originally exited. Reinforce.

SWIRL BRACELET

Bead chains are used in this complex-looking design as the sides of the bracelet. Make several bracelets in coordinating colors to wear together.

Materials

size 12 beading needle

size D Nymo thread

twenty-six 4mm fire polish beads

one 8mm round bead

6 grams size 11 Japanese seed beads for main color

3 grams size 15 Japanese seed beads for first accent color

1 gram size 8 Japanese seed beads for second accent color

TWO STARS ✹ ✹

Chain pattern 1

Start with approximately 2yd. (2m) of thread, single thickness with no knot. Pick up six size 15 beads and go through all six beads again from the tail end. This creates a small circle. Leave a 4"–6" (10cm–15cm) tail.

Chain pattern 2

Pick up five size 15 beads and go back through the sixth bead of the original circle. Go through the first three beads of the five just picked up. (You are going through a total of four beads.) Go through the beads on the opposite side from where the thread originally exited. Pull snug.

Pick up five size 15 beads and go back through the bead the working thread is coming out of on the opposite side and also go through the first three beads of the five just picked up. Pull snug.

Repeat this step to continue making circles until you have fifty-three circles. (Make a few less circles or a few more to vary the length if needed.) Fifty-three circles will make a bracelet that is approximately 7¹/₂" (19cm) long.

Repeat chain pattern 1–2 to make another chain the same length. You need two chains for your bracelet. Tie off the working and tail threads on both chains.

Chain pattern 3

Start a new thread that is approximately 2yd. (2m) long, single thickness with no knot.

Pick up one size 11 bead and turn it into a stopper bead by going back through it from the tail end. Leave an 8"–10" (20cm–25cm) tail.

Go through the first circle of one of the chains. Pick up one size 11 bead, one size 8 bead and one size 11 bead and go through the first circle of the second chain.

Chain pattern 4

Pick up five size 11 beads and go through the next circle of the chain the thread is exiting from. Pick up one 4mm fire polish bead. Go through the next circle of the opposite chain. The bead chains are held horizontally in place between the swirls of beads that are being added.

Chain pattern 5

Pick up five size 11 beads and go through the next circle of the chain. Pick up one size 11 bead, one size 8 bead and one size 11 bead and go through the next circle of the opposite chain.

Keep working back and forth through the circles of the chain in this way. There should always be five size 11 beads on the outside edges of the chain and the inside beads should alternate between the size 11, size 8 and size 11 combination and the 4mm fire polish beads.

Chain pattern 6

At the end of the chain, pick up one size 11 bead instead of five for the loop outside the chain. Skip that bead and go through one of the size 15 beads of the chain (this is to anchor the bead).

Go through the last group of inside beads and come out of the circle on the chain.

Chain pattern 7

Pick up five size 11 beads, the 8mm bead and three size 11 beads. Skip the three size 11 beads and go back down the 8mm bead and the next size 11 bead.

Pick up four size 11 beads and go through the circle of the chain and the center beads on the opposite side from where the thread originally exited. Reinforce.

Chain pattern 8

To add the loop end on the opposite side, weave the tail thread (from chain pattern 3) so it is coming out of the circle on the chain at the end of the strap.

Pick up five size 11 beads. Pick up enough size 11 beads to fit comfortable but snugly around the 8mm bead. Go through fifth size 11 bead of the first group of beads you added. Pick up four size 11 beads and go through the circle of the chain and the center beads on the opposite side from where the thread originally exited. Reinforce.

Tie off any remaining threads.

47

VICTORIAN CABOCHON NECKLACE & EARRINGS

I had hoarded boxes of crystals—pear-shaped ones—and decided I needed to do something with them. I love Victorian jewelry and will often design pieces that reflect that era. Picot stitches and size 15 seed beads give this necklace a delicate quality. The dangle earrings are lightweight and look great with an evening outfit.

Necklace Materials

size 12 beading needle

size D Nymo thread

one 18mm × 13mm pear-shaped crystal

five main color 4mm bicone crystals

five accent color 4mm bicone crystals

three drop beads

one 8mm round bead

12 grams size 15 Japanese seed beads for main color

small piece of interfacing

small piece of suede or ultrasuede

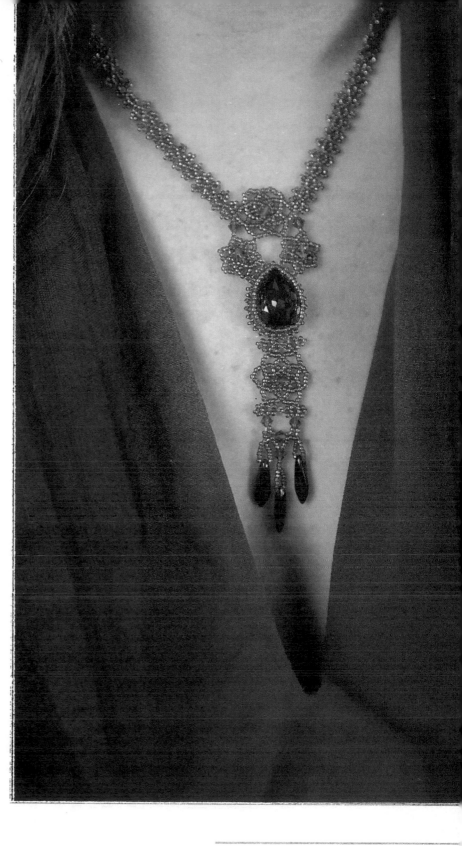

Earring Materials

size 12 beading needle

size D Nymo thread

four main color 4mm bicone crystals

six accent color 4mm bicone crystals

six drop beads

pair of earwires

5 grams size 15 Japanese seed beads for main color

TWO STARS

Bezel pattern 1

Adhere the 18mm × 13mm crystal to the interfacing (see *Adhesive Basics for Bead Embroidery* on page 20). Make sure the crystal is held firmly in place and is attached as close to the edges as possible.

Starting with approximately 2yd. (2m) of thread, single thickness with a knot at the end, stitch the first row of bead embroidery (see *Backstitch for Bead Embroidery* on page 21). Work the backstitch until you have gone all the way around the crystal. You must end with an even number of beads, so watch the spacing at the end to ensure you use an even number of beads.

Bezel pattern 2

The working thread should be coming out of one of the backstitch beads. Pick up one main color bead, skip the next bead of the backstitch row and go through the next one. This is peyote stitch.

Repeat this pattern around the crystal. Try to keep the new beads on top of the previous backstitch row. This row will look a little messy. Pull snug.

Bezel pattern 3

When you get to the end of the row, you have to do a step up before starting the next row. To do this, go through the first bead of the row just added before you start the next row.

Work one more row of peyote (pick up a bead, skip a bead and go through the next one). Pull snug. This completes the bezel around the crystal.

Bezel pattern 4

Trim away the excess interfacing. Trim as close to the beads as possible, being very careful not to cut any threads. Use glue or double-sided tape to attach the crystal to a piece of suede.

Trim the suede to match the interfacing. Weave the working thread so it is coming out at the edge of the suede. Pick up three main color beads and go through the suede about a bead's width over from where the thread originally exited. Go back up the third bead picked up from the bottom up. This creates a picot.

Bezel pattern 5

Pick up two main color beads and go through the suede about a bead's width over from the last stitch. Go back up the second bead. The two beads just added will sit on the previous stitch and create another picot.

Bezel pattern 6

Repeat bezel pattern 5 until you have gone all the way around the beadwork.

For the last stitch, only one bead is needed to finish the row. Pick up one bead and go down the first bead of the edging, catch the suede and come back up the same bead.

Accent pattern 1

Start a new thread, approximately 2yd. (2m), single thickness with no knot. Pick up twelve main color beads and go back through all of them again from the tail end. Go through the next bead to pull the circle tighter. Leave a 4"–6" (10cm–15cm) tail

Pick up three main color beads, skip the next bead of the circle and go through the bead after that. This creates a picot or point.

Accent pattern 2

Repeat accent pattern 1 until there are six points.

On the last point, go through the first two beads of the first point created in this row. This lines you up to start the next row.

Accent pattern 3

Pick up five main color beads and go through the middle bead of the next point from the last row (the second bead).

Accent pattern 4

Repeat accent pattern 3 until there are six more points.

On the last point, go through the first three beads of the first point of this row.

Accent pattern 5

Pick up seven main color beads and go through the middle bead (the third bead) of the next point from the previous row.

Accent pattern 6

Repeat accent pattern 5 until there are six more points. After the last point, weave down to the original circle of twelve beads.

Pick up one main color bead, one main color crystal and one main color bead. Go through a bead of the original circle that is across from where the thread originally exited. This will make the crystal lay in the center of the netting.

Repeat accent pattern 1-6 to make one more netted piece this size. You need two for the necklace.

Accent pattern 7

Repeat accent pattern 1-4 to make two smaller netted pieces with the last rows containing five bead points. Add a main color crystal in the center of both of these netted pieces as described in accent pattern 6.

Weave in and tie off your tail threads but leave the working threads on all four pieces.

Assembly 1

Find the four center bottom beads (approximately, they probably won't be perfectly aligned) of the edging beads that are sticking out on your crystal. Weave the working thread of one of the large netted pieces so it comes out of a middle bead of a point of the last row.

Pick up three main color beads and go through the first edging bead of the four center beads on the bottom of the crystal. Pick up three main color beads and go back through the middle bead of the point on the opposite side from where the thread originally exited.

Assembly 2

Come out of the middle bead of the three beads that connect the netted piece to the crystal. Pick up three main color beads and go back through the middle bead on the opposite side from where the thread originally exited. This creates a picot.

Assembly 3

Repeat assembly 2 on the remaining three beads from assembly 1 that connect the two pieces.

Assembly 4

Weave over to the fourth center bead of the edging on the bottom of the crystal. Repeat assembly 1–3 to completely connect the two pieces.

Sew the inside picots together at the middle beads using a circular thread path.

Fringe pattern 1

Weave the working thread (you need approximately 18" [46cm] of thread) down to the middle bead of the point of the last row of the netted piece that is across from the connection to the crystal.

Pick up three main color beads, one 4mm accent crystal, three main color beads, one 4mm main crystal, three main color beads, one 4mm accent crystal and three more main color beads. Go through the middle bead of the next point.

Pick up three main color beads and go through the last 4mm accent crystal that was picked up.

Pick up nine main color beads, a drop bead and six more main color beads. Go up through the third main color bead of the nine picked up previously.

Pick up two main color beads and go through the 4mm main crystal.

Fringe pattern 2

Pick up three main color beads, one accent crystal, nine main color beads, a drop bead and six main color beads. Go up through the first three main color beads of the nine and also go through the accent crystal.

Pick up three main color beads and go through the 4mm main crystal on the opposite side from where the thread originally exited.

Fringe pattern 3

Pick up nine main color beads, a drop bead and six main color beads. Go up through the third main color bead of the nine.

Pick up two main color beads and go up through the first 4mm accent crystal.

Pick up three main color crystals and go through the middle point bead your thread originally exited from on the opposite side.

Fringe pattern 4

Weave down to the middle bead of the three main color beads below the point.

Pick up three main color beads and go back through the main color bead your thread exited from on the opposite side. This creates a picot. Make another picot on the other set of three main color beads next to the first picot.

Weave over to the next set of three main color beads below the other point and repeat the picots. Circle stitch (see *Circle Stitch* page 13) the center picots together.

Assembly 5

Weave a working thread of one of the smaller netted pieces so it is coming out of the middle bead of a point of the last row. Using a circle stitch (see *Circle Stitch* on page 13), attach the smaller netted piece to a bead of the outside edging that is sticking out at the top of the crystal. Reinforce.

Assembly 6

Weave over to the middle bead of the next point of the netted piece and attach it to the crystal at the closest edging bead (it is usually the fourth bead away from the first connection, but depending on your spacing, it may be different) by using a circle stitch. Reinforce.

Assembly 7

Repeat assembly 5–6 to attach the remaining small netted piece on the other side of the crystal.

Assembly 8

Weave the working thread from one of the small netted pieces so it is coming out of the middle bead of the next point up from where it was just connected to the crystal. Using a circle stitch, attach the small netted piece to a middle bead of the point of the last row of the second large netted piece. Reinforce.

Weave over to the next point of the large netted piece and attach the middle point bead to the middle point bead of the other smaller netted piece. Reinforce.

Assembly 9

Weave a working thread so it is coming out of the middle point bead of a smaller netted piece.

Pick up one main color bead, one 4mm accent crystal and one main color bead. Go through the middle bead of the next point of the larger netted piece at the next point. Reinforce with a circle stitch.

Repeat on the other side of the crystal. Reinforce.

Strap pattern 1

Weave the working thread so it is coming out of the middle point bead of the larger netted piece where the accent crystal was just added.

Pick up seven main color beads and go back through the bead the thread originally exited from on the opposite side. Also go through the first two beads of the seven just added. This makes a small circle.

Pick up three main color beads and go back through the bead the thread originally exited from on the opposite side. This creates a picot.

Needle over to the sixth bead of the seven beads and create another picot on the other side of the small circle of seven beads.

Strap pattern 2

Weave the working thread so it is coming out of the fourth bead of the seven bead circle. Repeat strap pattern 1 until the strap is the desired length. A good approximate length is 7"-8" (18cm-20cm) long.

Strap pattern 3

Weave the working thread so it is coming out of the fourth bead of the last circle of the strap.

Pick up four main color beads, the 8mm bead and three more main color beads. Skip the last three main color beads and go back through the 8mm bead and the next main color bead.

Pick up three more main color beads and go through the bead the thread originally exited from on the opposite side. Reinforce.

Strap pattern 4

Repeat strap pattern 1-2 on the other side of the large netted piece until the straps are of equal length. Make a loop of main color beads that fits snugly but comfortably over the clasp bead. Tie off any remaining threads.

EARRINGS

Earrings pattern

Follow accent pattern 1–6 (pages 51–52) of the Victorian Cabochon Necklace to make one netted piece. Then follow fringe pattern 1–4 (page 54) for the fringe.

Weave the working thread so it is coming out of the middle bead of one of the points of the last row of points of the netted piece that is centered above your fringe. Pick up thirteen main color beads and go back through the seventh bead of the thirteen that was just picked up.

Pick up six main color beads and go through the middle point bead of the next point at the top of the earring. Reinforce. Tie off any remaining threads.

Attach the ear wire to the beaded piece by first opening the loop at the bottom of the ear wire. Thread the top loop of the piece onto the ear wire loop, then close the ear wire loop.

Repeat for the other earring.

REVERSIBLE PENDANT LARIAT

The pendant ends of the lariat look pretty no matter which side is showing. Make the lariat as long or as short as you want and experiment with different ways to wear it.

Materials

size 12 beading needle

size D Nymo thread

two 18mm crystal rivolis

two 12mm crystals or beads (a flatter, aspirin shape works best)

two 4mm crystal sequins

two drop beads

40 grams size 15 Japanese seed beads

8 grams size 11 Japanese seed beads for main color

4 grams size 11 Japanese seed beads for accent color

4 grams size 11 Japanese delica beads

 **THREE STARS**

Pendant pattern 1

Start with approximately 2yd. (2m) of thread, single thickness with no knot. Pick up three accent beads and go back through them again from the tail end. This creates a small triangle. Leave a 4"-6" (10cm-15cm) tail.

Pendant pattern 2

Pick up two main color beads and go through the next accent bead. Repeat two more times. There are a total of six beads in this row.

After adding the last two beads, go through the first main color bead that was added in this row. This lines the thread up to start the next row.

Pendant pattern 3

Pick up one accent bead and go through the next main color bead. Repeat five more times. There are a total of six beads in this row.

After adding the last bead, go through the first accent bead that was added in this row.

Pendant pattern 4

Pick up two main color beads and go through the next accent bead. Repeat five more times. There are a total of twelve beads in this row.

After adding the last two beads, go through the first main color bead that was added in this row.

Pendant pattern 5

Pick up one accent bead and go through the next main color bead. Repeat eleven more times. There are a total of twelve beads in this row.

After adding the last bead, go through the first accent bead added in this row.

Pendant pattern 6

Pick up one main color bead and go through the next accent bead. Repeat eleven more times. There are a total of twelve beads in this row.

After adding the last bead, go through the first main color bead added in this row.

Pendant pattern 7

Pick up one accent bead and go through the next main color bead. Repeat eleven more times. There are a total of twelve beads in this row.

After adding the last bead, go through the first accent bead added in this row.

Pendant pattern 8

Pick up two main color beads and go through the next accent bead. Repeat eleven more times. There are a total of twenty-four beads in this row.

After adding the last two beads, go through the first two main color beads added in this row.

Pendant pattern 9

Pick up one accent bead and go through the next two main color beads. Repeat eleven more times. There are a total of twelve beads in this row.

After adding the last bead, go through the first accent bead added in this row.

Pendant pattern 10

Pick up three main color beads and go through the next accent bead. Repeat eleven more times. There are a total of thirty-six beads in this row.

After adding the last three main color beads, go through the first two main color beads added in this row.

Pendant pattern 11

Pick up three main color beads and go through the second bead of the next set of three beads from pendant pattern 10.

Pick up one size 15 bead, one main color bead and one size 15 bead. Go through the second bead of the next set of three beads.

Pendant pattern 12

Repeat pendant pattern 11, alternating between three main color beads and the size 15 beads with a main color bead until you have gone all the way around the circle. It should take twelve sets of beads. Pull this row snug. The circle should start to curl up at the edge.

After the twelve sets of beads are added, go through the first two beads of the first three beads added in this row.

Pendant pattern 13

Pick up five main color beads, skip over the next set of three beads and go through the second bead of the next set. Pull snug. Repeat all the way around. There should be six sets of five beads.

When you get to the last set of five beads, insert the 18mm crystal and pull the thread snug. Reinforce this row.

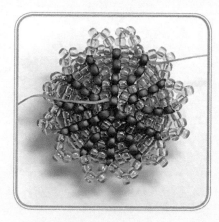

Pendant pattern 14

Flip the piece over so the beaded pattern side is showing. Weave the working thread so it is coming out of an accent bead from pendant pattern 9.

Pick up five main color beads and go through the next accent bead in the row from pendant pattern 9. Repeat all the way around. This creates a row of points around the crystal.

Pendant pattern 15

Put a needle on the tail thread. It should be coming out of an accent bead of the first row from pendant pattern 1.

Pick up the 4mm crystal sequin and one size 15 bead. Skip the size 15 bead and go back through the sequin. Go through the accent bead across from where the thread originally exited. The sequin should sit in the middle of the beadwork.

Weave the tail thread in and tie it off, leaving the working thread attached. Repeat pendant pattern 1–15 to create a second large pendant.

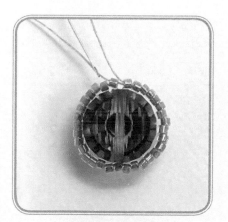

Small pendant pattern 1

Start a new thread, approximately 1 1/2 yd. (1.5m) of thread, single thickness with no knot.

Pick up sixteen delica beads and go through the 12mm crystal. Go back through all the beads again from the tail end. Leave a 4"–6" (10cm–15cm) tail.

Pick up sixteen more delica beads and go back through the crystal on the opposite side from where the thread originally exited. Go back through all the delica beads again to pull them tighter around the crystal.

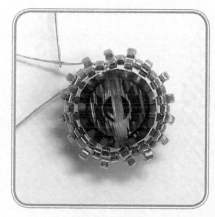

Small pendant pattern 2

The working thread should be coming out of one of the delica beads. Pick up one delica bead, skip over one and go through the next one (peyote stitch). Repeat all the way around the original circle of delica beads. There will be a total of sixteen beads.

After you add the last bead, go through the first bead that was added in this row.

Small pendant pattern 3

Pick up one delica bead and go through the bead that sticks up. Repeat all the way around. There will be a total of sixteen beads.

After you add the last bead, go through the first bead that was added in this row. Make sure to pull this row snug. The beads should be sitting snugly around the edge of the crystal.

Small pendant pattern 4

Do two more rows of peyote using the size 15 beads. Be sure to pull the thread snug. This will pull in the beadwork so it fits snugly around the crystal.

Weave the working thread over to the other side of the crystal and come out of one of the delica beads that are sticking out. Do two rows of peyote stitch with the size 15 beads on this side. If your crystal (or bead) is on the wide side, do an extra row or two of peyote with the size 15 beads. This will help to pull the beadwork in more snugly.

Weave in and tie off the tail thread, leaving the working thread attached. Repeat small pendant pattern 1–4 to create a second small pendant.

Assembly 1

Put a needle on the working thread on one of the large pendant pieces. The thread should be coming out of the third bead of one of the points.

Pick up one main color bead, one accent bead and one more main color bead. Go through one of the delica beads on one of the small pendants that is sitting in a little more. The pendants should both have the crystals facing out.

Pick up one main color bead and go back up the accent bead. Pick up one main color bead and go through the point bead the thread originally exited from on the opposite side.

Assembly 2

Weave over to the next point and repeat assembly 1. On the small pendant, skip a delica and go through the next one that is sitting in a little more and is parallel with the first delica you went through. Tie off the working thread from the large pendant.

Assembly 3

Put a needle on the working thread from the small pendant. Weave the thread down to the bottom of the crystal and come out of the delica that is the most centered below the connection of the two crystals.

Pick up one main bead, one accent bead, one main bead, one drop bead and four accent beads. Skip the last three accent beads and go back up the first accent bead and the drop bead.

Pick up one main color bead and go through the accent bead. Then pick up one main color bead and go through the delica bead the thread originally exited from on the opposite side. Weave the working thread in and tie it off.

Repeat assembly 1–3 to connect the two remaining pendants.

Rope pattern 1

Start a new thread, approximately 2yd. (2m), single thickness with no knot. Pick up fourteen size 15 beads. Tie them into a circle. Leave a 10"–12" (25cm–30cm) tail.

Pick up three size 15 beads, skip over the three beads and go through the fourth bead.

Rope pattern 2

Repeat the pattern in rope pattern 1 two more times. Pull the beads snug. They need to sit on top of the original circle.

Rope pattern 3

Pick up three size 15 beads and go through the second bead from the first set of beads that were added in the last row.

The rope continually spirals; there is no step up at the end of each row. Continuously pull the beads snug.

Rope pattern 4

Keep picking up three beads, skipping three beads and going through the second bead of the next group of three beads. The middle bead of the three that are skipped will be recessed. The photo shows the rope in progress.

A good approximate length for the rope is 28" (71cm).

Assembly 4

After you have the rope the desired length, you can add the pendants. The working thread should be coming out of a bead at the end of the rope. Weave through the end beads to pull the beads in tighter.

Pick up one accent bead and go through the third bead of a point across from the connections of the crystals. Go back through the accent bead and the bead of the rope that your thread originally exited from on the opposite side.

Weave over to a bead at the end of the rope that is across from this first connection and repeat on the next point of the crystal. Put a needle on the tail thread at the other end of the rope and repeat with the other pendant.

Tie off any remaining threads.

PEARL AND CRYSTAL BRACELET

I love the look of wide bracelets and cuffs, but I also like my jewelry to be delicate. I think this bracelet manages to be both of those things. It is light enough to wear all day and dressy enough to go into the evening.

Materials

size 12 beading needle

size D Nymo thread

thirty-four 4mm
bicone crystals

ninety-nine 3mm
glass pearls

two 4mm round beads

two grams size 8
Japanese hex beads

9 grams size 15 Japanese
seed beads for main color

6 grams size 11 Japanese
seed beads for accent color

  TWO STARS

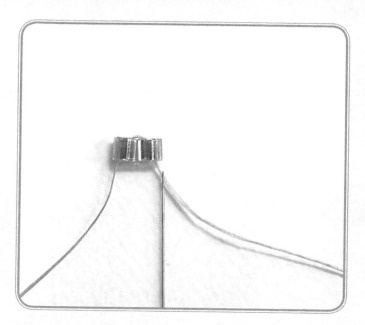

Bracelet pattern 1

Start with approximately 2½yd. (2.5m) of thread, single thickness with no knot.

Pick up two hex beads and go back through both beads again from the tail end. This will make the two beads sit side by side.

Bracelet pattern 2

Pick up one hex bead and go back through the bead the thread is exiting from on the opposite side and also go through the bead just picked up. This will make the new bead sit next to the previous beads. Repeat until you have a total of twelve hex beads side by side.

Start another thread (approximately 2½yd. [2.5m] long) and make another piece of beadwork just like the first piece. Two pieces with twelve beads side by side are needed for the bracelet.

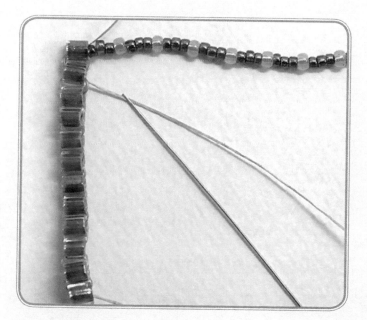

Bracelet pattern 3

With one of the working threads on one of the pieces, pick up three main color beads and one accent bead. Keep picking up three main color beads and one accent bead until you have enough beads to just about meet around your wrist. (For a 7½" [19cm] bracelet, you will need thirty-four sets of main color beads.) Start and end with a set of three main color beads.

After the beads are picked up, go through the first or end bead of the other hex piece. Go through the second or next hex bead so the working thread is going toward the sets of main color beads.

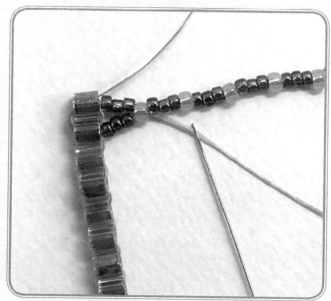

Bracelet pattern 4

Pick up three main color beads and go through the next accent bead. Repeat until you have gone all the way back down the sets of main color beads. Pull the beads snug.

After adding the last set of three main color beads, go through the second hex bead and then come back down the third hex bead. This lines you up for the next pass of beads.

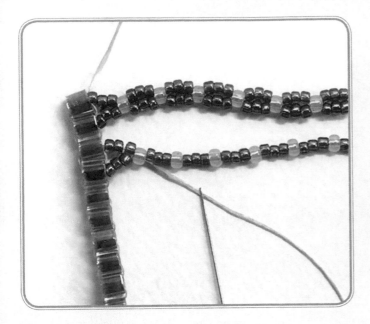

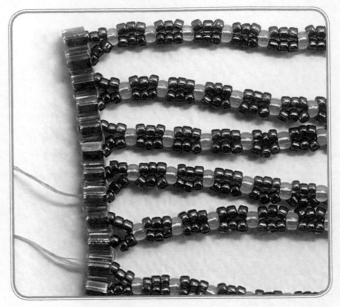

Bracelet pattern 5

Pick up three main color beads and one accent bead. Repeat until you have the same number of sets of main color beads as you did in your first row of beads.

After the beads are picked up, go through the third hex bead at the other end of the bracelet. Go through the fourth hex bead so the thread is going toward the sets of main color beads.

Pick up three main color beads and go through the next accent bead. Repeat until you have gone back down all the sets of main color beads.

Bracelet pattern 6

Repeat bracelet pattern 3-5 until you have a total of six beaded rows.

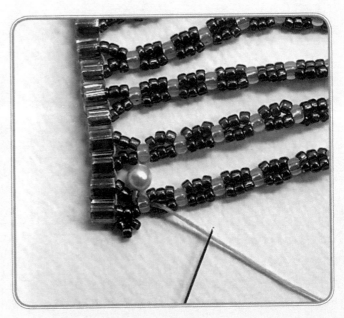

Bracelet pattern 7

Weave a working thread (you need approximately 24"-36" [61cm-91cm] of thread) so it is coming out of the second main color bead of the first set of three main color beads on the outside edge.

Pick up three main color beads and go back through the main color bead the thread originally exited from on the opposite side. This creates a picot.

Bracelet pattern 8

Go through the third main color bead of the set of three and come out of the accent bead. Pick up one 3mm pearl and go through the corresponding accent bead of the next chain.

Go back through the pearl and go back through the accent bead your thread originally exited from on the opposite side. Come out of the second main color bead of the next set of three main color beads on the outside edge.

Repeat bracelet pattern 7-8 (making picots and adding pearls) until you get to the end of the chain. The last set of three main color beads should end with a picot.

Bracelet pattern 9

Weave a working thread so it is coming out of the second bead of the second set of three main color beads on the second chain on the inside.

Pick up one 4mm crystal go through the corresponding main color bead of the next chain. Go back through the crystal and the main color bead your thread originally exited from on the opposite side.

Bracelet pattern 10

The crystals are only added on every other set of main color beads.

Weave the working thread so it is coming out of the second bead of the second set of main color beads after the first crystal. Add another crystal in the same way as you added the first crystal.

Keep adding crystals until you get to the end of the chain.

Bracelet pattern 11

Weave the thread so it is coming out of the accent bead of the next set of chains.

Add 3mm pearls at the accent bead like you did in bracelet pattern 8. However, this time there will not be any picots added because it is the middle row of pearls.

Bracelet pattern 12

Weave the working thread over to the next set of chains and add another row of 4mm crystals just like you added in bracelet pattern 10. This row of crystals should line up with the row you added in bracelet pattern 10. If the first row ended with a crystal at the last three main color beads, start with a crystal across from it.

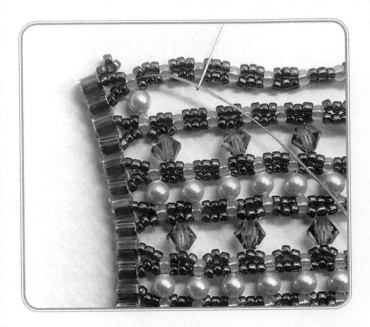

Bracelet pattern 13

Weave over to the next chain. Repeat bracelet pattern 7–8 to add the last row of picots and 3mm pearls .

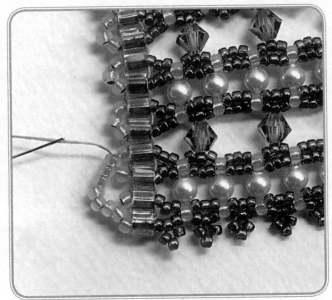

Closure pattern 1

Weave the working thread so it is coming out of the end hex bead at one end of the bracelet, going away from the beadwork.

Pick up three accent beads and go down the second hex bead and come back up the third hex bead. Repeat all the way across the hex beads. There should be six points.

Closure pattern 2

Weave the working thread so it is coming out of the second accent bead of the point on one end of the bracelet.

Pick up five accent beads and go through the second accent bead of the next point. Repeat four more times. There should be five points on this row.

Closure pattern 3

Weave the thread so it is coming out of the third accent bead of the second point. Pick up three accent beads, one main color bead, one 4mm bead and three more main color beads. Skip the three main color beads and go back down the 4mm bead and the next main color bead.

Pick up three accent beads and go back through the accent bead of the point that the thread originally exited from on the opposite side. Reinforce.

Closure pattern 4

Weave over and come out of the third accent bead of the fourth point and repeat the bead pattern in closure pattern 3. Reinforce.

Closure pattern 5

Repeat closure pattern 1–4 for on the other end of the bracelet. However, instead of adding two 4mm beads for the clasp, add two small loops that fit snugly but comfortably over the 4mm beads. Tie off any remaining threads.

SCALLOPED LACE NECKLACE

The netted pieces of this necklace remind me of the lace doilies my grandmother crocheted. The pearls and crystals add an elegant touch to its vintage appeal.

Materials

size 12 beading needle

size D Nymo thread

forty-three 4mm glass pearls

thirty-one 4mm bicone crystals

one drop bead

one 8mm round bead

12 grams size 15 Japanese seed beads for main color

 TWO STARS

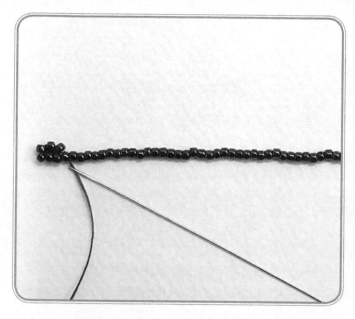

Scallop pattern 1

Start with approximately 1½ yd. (1.5m) of thread, single thickness with no knot. Pick up one main color bead and turn it into a stopper bead by going back through it from the tail end. Leave a 4"–6" (10cm–15cm) tail.

Pick up fifty main color beads for a total of fifty one beads. Go back through the forty-fifth bead going toward the tail end. This makes a small circle at the end of the beads.

Scallop pattern 2

Pick up three main color beads, skip over the next three main color beads and go through the next main color bead. Repeat until you get to the end of the original fifty one beads.

For the last loop, pick up three main color beads and go through the second and third bead of the original fifty one beads. This makes a small circle at the end.

The stopper bead is not part of the pattern; pull it off. There should now be twelve circles.

Scallop pattern 3

Pick up five main color beads and go through the second bead of the next set of three main color beads on the side of the circle. This will make a point. Repeat until you get to the end of the circles.

The beadwork will start to curve. On the last circle, go through the second bead of the last set of three main color beads and also through the first three beads of the five main color beads you just added.

Scallop pattern 4

Pick up five main color beads and go through the third main color bead of the next point of five main color beads created in the last row. Repeat until you get to the end of the row.

At the end of the row, go through the third main color bead and also through the next five main color beads.

71

Scallop pattern 5

Pick up one 4mm crystal, one main color bead, one 4mm glass pearl, one main color bead and one 4mm crystal. Go through the third bead from the connection on the inside of the other end of the beadwork.

Go back through the last 4mm crystal, the next main color bead and the 4mm pearl.

Scallop pattern 6

Pick up seven main color beads and go back through the 4mm pearl on the opposite side from where the thread originally exited. Go through the first two main color beads.

Scallop pattern 7

Pick up three main color beads and go back through the main color bead the thread originally exited from on the opposite side. This creates a picot.

Go through the next two main color beads of the seven around the pearl. Pick up three more main color beads and make another picot.

Weave the thread around to the center bead of the picot just created. Pick up one main color bead, one 4mm crystal and then four more main color beads. Skip the last three main color beads and go up the first main color bead of the four and also go up through the crystal. This will make a picot under the crystal.

Pick up one main color bead and go through the middle picot bead your thread originally exited from on the opposite side. Weave the working thread so it is coming out of the second-to-last main color bead of the original seven and create another picot with three main color beads.

Weave through the seventh main color bead, the 4mm pearl, the next main color bead, the 4mm crystal and the next five main color beads. Weave in the tail thread but leave the working thread attached.

Repeat scallop pattern 1–7 to create seven more netted pieces. There are eight total for the necklace.

Assembly 1

Put a needle on the working thread from one of the netted pieces. It should be coming out of the five main color beads at the end.

Pick up one main color bead, one 4mm pearl and one more main color bead. Go through the five main color beads on the end of another netted piece. Go through the 4mm crystal, main color bead, 4mm pearl, main color bead, 4mm crystal and the next five main color beads.

Repeat until five netted pieces are connected.

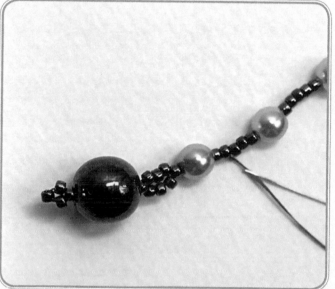

Chain pattern 1

The working thread should now be coming out of the five main color beads of the last netted piece. (If the thread is not very long, start a new thread approximately 1¹/₂yd. [1.5m] and weave it so it is coming out of the five main color beads at the end.)

Pick up one 4mm pearl and then five main color beads. Repeat until you have fourteen of the pearls picked up with five main color beads between each pearl. End with five main color beads.

Pick up the 8mm bead and four main color beads. Skip the last three main color beads and go back through the first main color bead, the 8mm bead and the next main color bead.

Pick up three main color beads and go through the last main color bead of the set of five added previously, the pearl and the next main color bead.

Repeat adding three main color beads and going through the last main color bead of the five, the pearl and the next main color bead until you get back to the netted piece.

Chain pattern 2

Weave the working thread around so it is coming out of the third main color bead after the first 4mm pearl of the strap. Pick up three main color beads and go back through the main color bead the thread originally exited from on the opposite side. This creates a picot.

Weave up to the third bead of the next set of five beads and repeat. Repeat this pattern until you reach the end of the strap.

Chain pattern 3

Weave the working thread through the end beads and come out of the third main color bead on the other side from where the last picot was created.

Pick up three main color beads and go back through the main color bead the thread originally exited from on the opposite side. This creates another picot across from the one previously made. Repeat making these picots until the other half of the strap has picots.

Repeat chain pattern 1–3 on the other side for the second half of the strap; however, instead of adding an 8mm bead, add a loop of main color beads that fits comfortably but snugly over the clasp bead.

Assembly 2

Weave a working thread left earlier so it is coming out of the third bead of the last row on the third point on the inside of the first netted piece.

Pick up one 4mm crystal, one main color bead, one 4mm pearl, one main color bead and one more 4mm crystal. Go through the third bead of the third point of the next netted piece.

Go back through the beads just added and also go back through the main color bead of the point the thread originally exited from on the opposite side.

Repeat this step on the fourth and fifth netted pieces.

Assembly 3

Pick up an unattached netted piece. The working thread should be coming out of the five main color beads at the end.

Circle stitch (see *Circle Stitch* on page 13) the fifth main color bead to the recessed bead between the third and fourth point on the inside of the second netted piece.

Assembly 4

Weave the working thread so it is coming out of the fifth main color bead on the other side of the netted piece. Circle stitch the netted piece to the recessed bead between the fourth and fifth points on the inside of the third netted piece.

Repeat assembly 3-4 on the other side of the necklace with another netted piece. There should be two netted pieces attached underneath the five netted pieces.

Assembly 6

The working thread of the last unattached netted piece should be coming out of the five end main color beads.

Circle stitch the final netted piece to the recessed bead between the third and fourth point on the inside of the first netted piece added in assembly 3.

Weave over and circle stitch the fifth main color bead on the other end to the recessed bead between the third and fourth points on the next netted piece.

Assembly 7

Weave a working thread (you need approximately 10" [25cm] of thread) down to the third bead of the fifth point on the last netted piece added.

Pick up five main color beads, one 4mm crystal, one main color bead, one 4mm pearl, one main color bead, one 4mm crystal, one main color bead, the drop bead, one 4mm crystal and four main color beads.

Skip the last three main color beads and go up the next main color bead and the other beads until you get up to the fifth main color bead of the first five that were added. Go through the fifth bead and then pick up four main color beads and go through the third bead of the next point of the last netted piece.

Reinforce the fringe one time. It should be centered under the last netted piece. Weave in any remaining threads.

PEARL DAISY BRACELET

This bracelet was inspired by a photo of an antique bangle bracelet. It was a delicate piece that I thought would translate well with beads. After fiddling with a few ideas, this was the final design.

Materials

size 12 beading needle

size D Nymo thread

two 8mm flat crystals

thirteen 4mm glass pearls

forty-two 3mm glass pearls

4 grams size 15 Japanese seed beads for main color

 **ONE STAR**

Chain pattern 1

Start with 2½yd. (2.5cm) of thread, single thickness with no knot.

Pick up one 8mm crystal and six 3mm pearls. Go back through the crystal and the pearls from the tail end. Go back through the crystal one more time.

Leave approximately half the thread as your tail. This will be used later.

Chain pattern 2

Pick up six 3mm pearls and go back through the crystal on the opposite side from where the thread exited.

Go through all the pearls to pull them in closer to the crystal.

Chain pattern 3

The working thread should be coming out of one 3mm pearl. Pick up five size 15 beads, skip over the next 3mm pearl and go through the next one.

Chain pattern 4

Repeat chain pattern 3 five more times. There should be six points around the pearls.

After you make the sixth point, go through the first three size 15 beads of the first point you created. This lines the thread up for the next step.

Chain pattern 5

Pick up twelve size 15 beads, one 4mm pearl and twelve size 15 beads. Go back through the size 15 bead of the point that the thread originally exited from on the opposite side. Also go back through the first twelve size 15 beads and the 4mm pearl.

Chain pattern 6

Pick up two 4mm pearls and go back through the pearl the thread originally exited from on the opposite side.

Chain pattern 7

Go through the next 4mm pearl. Pick up nine size 15 beads and go back through the pearl on the opposite side from where the thread originally exited.

Chain pattern 8

Go through the next 4mm pearl and repeat chain pattern 7.

Chain pattern 9

Weave the working thread so it is coming out of the seventh size 15 bead of the last nine beads that were added around the 4mm pearl.

Pick up seven size 15 beads and go back through the size 15 bead the thread originally exited from on the opposite side. Go through the first four size 15 beads that were just added. This makes a small circle.

Pick up seven size 15 beads and repeat this step.

Chain pattern 10

Put the needle on the long tail thread that was left in chain pattern 1. Weave the thread so it comes out of the third bead of the point of size 15 beads opposite the beadwork just created.

Chain pattern 11

Repeat chain pattern 5–9; however, instead of creating two small circles like in chain pattern 9, you will create 5 small circles at the end of the beadwork.

Repeat chain pattern 1–11 to make a second piece of beadwork that matches the first piece. Two pieces are needed for the bracelet.

Assembly 1

Align the two pieces of beadwork to match the photo.

Weave one of the threads to the middle bead of the second point of size 15 beads of the bottom piece of beadwork. Go through the middle bead of the point of the other top piece of beadwork.

Go back through the middle point bead the thread originally exited from on the opposite side. Reinforce.

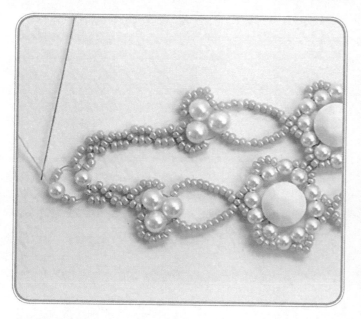

Assembly 2

Put the needle on a thread at the end of the beadwork. It should be coming out of the fourth bead of the last circle working toward the inside of the bracelet.

Pick up one 3mm pearl and go through the fourth bead of the last circle of the other piece of beadwork.

Pick up two size 15 beads, one 3mm pearl and two size 15 beads. Go back through the size 15 bead the thread originally exited from on the opposite side, weaving the thread through the beads to come out of the second 3mm pearl.

Assembly 3

Pick up seven size 15 beads, one 3mm pearl and seven size 15 beads. Go back through the 3mm pearl the thread originally exited from on the opposite side and also go through the first seven size 15 beads and the 3mm pearl that was added. This creates a circle.

Repeat this step until you have the desired number of circles at the end. The number you need is based on how long you want your bracelet to be.

Assembly 4

For the clasp bead, the working thread should be coming out of the end 3mm pearl. Pick up four size 15 beads, one 4mm pearl and three size 15 beads. Skip the last three size 15 beads and go back down the pearl and the next size 15 bead.

Pick up three more size 15 beads and go back through the 3mm pearl the thread originally exited on the opposite side. Reinforce.

Assembly 5

Repeat assembly 2-3 at the other end of the bracelet. The number of circles you create on this end should match the number of circles for assembly 4. Make a loop of size 15 beads that fits comfortably but snugly around the clasp bead. Reinforce.

Tie off any remaining threads.

CHARMING CHOKER

I love fringe—that's all there is
to it. I would fringe just about
every object in my home if I
didn't practice some restraint.
With this piece, I let my love of
fringe come out. It is a fun piece
to make and wear.

Materials

size 12 beading needle

size D Nymo thread

twelve 4mm fire polish
beads

one 6mm fire polish bead

twenty-five 4mm bicone
crystals

twenty-five drop beads

12 grams size 15 Japanese
seed beads for main color

6 grams size 15 Japanese
seed beads for accent color

5 grams size 11 Japanese
seed beads for accent color

 TWO STARS

Chain pattern 1

Start with 2yd. (2m) of thread, single thickness with no knot. Pick up five size 15 main color beads, one size 11 accent bead, five size 15 main color beads and one size 11 accent bead. Go back through the first five size 15 main color beads and the first size 11 accent bead you picked up from the tail end. This creates a small circle. Leave a 10"-12" (25cm–30cm) tail to use later.

Chain pattern 2

Pick up three size 15 main color beads and go back through the size 11 accent bead that the thread is exiting from on the opposite side. This makes a picot. Needle forward through the next three size 15 main color beads.

Chain pattern 3

Pick up three more size 15 main color beads and go back through the main color bead that the thread is exiting from on the opposite side.

Needle forward and come out of the next size 11 accent bead.

Chain pattern 4

Pick up three size 15 main color beads and go back through the size 11 accent bead that the thread is exiting from on the opposite side.

Needle forward through the next three size 15 main color beads.

Chain pattern 5

Now pick up three size 15 main color beads and go back through the size 15 main color bead that the thread is exiting from on the opposite side.

Go through the first two beads of the three you just picked up (come out of the center bead of the picot you just created).

Chain pattern 6

Pick up two size 15 main color beads, one size 11 accent bead and three size 15 main color beads. Go back through the size 11 accent bead on the opposite side. This creates a picot that will sit on top of the size 11 accent bead. Make sure this new segment of beads is pushed up snugly against the existing beads before you continue.

Chain pattern 7

Pick up six size 15 main color beads and go back through the third size 15 main color bead on the opposite side. This makes another picot. Pull snug.

Chain pattern 8

Pick up two size 15 main color beads, one size 11 accent bead and three size 15 main color beads. Go back through the size 11 bead on the opposite side. Pull snug.

Chain pattern 9

Pick up two size 15 main color beads and go back through the middle picot bead of the picot that the thread exited from when you started chain pattern 6. Go back through it on the opposite side from where the thread originally exited.

Chain pattern 10

Now weave the working thread so it is coming out of the middle picot bead across from the one you just went through. Two circles are connected side by side with picots.

Repeat chain pattern 6–10 until the beadwork is the desired length (this will be the top edge of the necklace band). **Note:** This piece must have an even number of circles. A good average length is forty-six circles.

Chain pattern 11

The working thread should be coming out of the end middle picot bead.

Pick up four size 11 accent beads, the 6mm bead and three size 11 accent beads. Skip the last three accent beads and go back through the 6mm bead and the next size 11 accent bead.

Pick up three more size 11 accent beads and go through the picot bead the thread originally exited on the opposite side. Reinforce this several times.

Chain pattern 12

Now put a needle on the tail thread left earlier. Weave it so it is coming out of the end middle picot bead. Then pick up enough size 11 accent beads to fit comfortably but snugly around the clasp bead. Reinforce this several times.

Repeat chain pattern 1–10 to make a second chain piece.

Note: The second chain piece must be one circle shorter than the top piece and it needs to be an odd number. If the top piece has forty-six circles, the bottom piece needs to have forty-five circles.

Assembly 1

After the second piece is completed, attach it to the top edge (the piece with the clasp bead).

Weave a working thread so it is coming out of the middle picot bead of the first picot on the side of the first piece of beadwork (it should be going in the direction of the beadwork). Pick up one size 15 main color bead, one size 11 accent bead and one size 15 main color bead. Go through the middle picot bead of the first picot on the side of the second piece of beadwork.

Assembly 2

Pick up one size 15 main color bead, one size 11 accent bead and one main color bead. Go through the middle picot bead of the next picot on the side of the top piece of beadwork.

Repeat this step until the two pieces of beadwork are sewn together.

Fringe pattern 1

Start a new thread, 1yd. (1m) long, single thickness with no knot. Pick up one 4mm bead and eight size 15 accent beads. Go back through the 4mm bead and the eight size 15 accent beads on the opposite side from where the thread is exiting. Leave a 4"–6" (10cm–15cm) tail.

Go back through the 4mm bead again. This makes the size 15 accent beads fit snugly against the 4mm bead.

Fringe pattern 2

Pick up eight size 15 accent beads and go back through the 4mm bead on the opposite side from where the thread originally exited.

Run the needle and thread through all of the size 15 accent beads to pull them snugly against the 4mm bead.

83

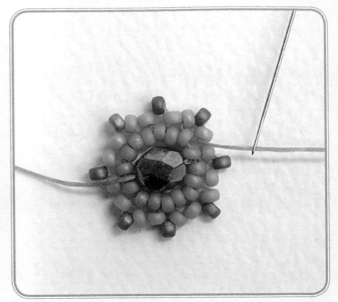

Fringe pattern 3

The thread should now be coming out of a size 15 accent bead. Pick up one size 15 accent bead, one size 15 main color bead and one size 15 accent bead. Go back through the size 15 accent bead the thread originally exited from on the opposite side.

Needle through the next two beads of the original circle of size 15 accent beads. This makes a picot and also lines you up to make the next picot.

Fringe pattern 4

Repeat fringe pattern 3 until you have a total of eight picots around the original circle.

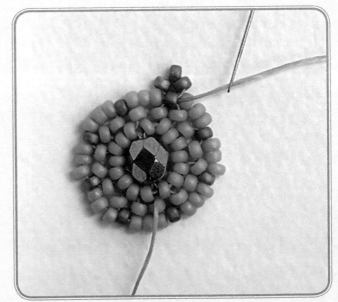

Fringe pattern 5

Weave the working thread so it is coming out of the size 15 main color bead of one of the picots (the middle bead). Pick up three size 15 accent beads and go through the size 15 main color bead of the next picot.

Fringe pattern 6

Repeat fringe pattern 5 until you have gone all the way around the piece, putting three size 15 accent beads between each picot.

The working thread should now be coming out of a size 15 main color bead (the center bead of the picots created earlier). Pick up three size 15 main color beads and go back through the bead the thread is exiting from on the opposite side. This creates a picot. Needle over to the next size 15 main color bead and create another picot.

Fringe pattern 7

Repeat fringe pattern 6 until you have gone all the way around and have eight picots.

Weave the working thread so it is coming out of the middle bead of one of the size 15 main color picots. Pick up three size 15 accent beads, one size 15 main color bead, one 4mm crystal, one size 15 main color bead, one drop bead and three size 15 main color beads. Skip the last three main color beads and go back up through the drop bead, the size 15 main color bead, the 4mm crystal and the next size 15 main color bead.

Pick up three size 15 accent beads and go back through the size 15 main color bead the thread originally exited from on the opposite side. Tie off the tail and working thread.

Repeat fringe pattern 1–7 to make eleven more charms, giving you a total of twelve charms for the choker.

Fringe pattern 8

There are thirteen pieces of straight fringe and twelve charms that hang from the choker, for a total of twenty-five fringes.

Find the center twenty-five picots on the bottom edge of the choker. Weave a new thread, approximately 2½yd. (2.5m) long, so it is coming out of the middle bead of the first picot of the fringe, going toward the middle of the choker.

Pick up six size 15 accent beads, one size 15 main color bead, one 4mm crystal, one size 15 main color bead, one drop bead and three size 15 main color beads. Skip the last three size 15 main color beads and go back up the drop bead, the size 15 main color bead, the 4mm crystal and the next size 15 main color bead.

Pick up six more size 15 accent beads and go back through the picot bead the thread originally exited from on the opposite side.

Fringe pattern 9

Weave the thread over to the next picot, come out of the middle bead and go through the top middle picot bead of one of the charms and go back through the picot bead the thread exited from on the opposite side.

Repeat fringe pattern 8–9, alternating between a straight fringe and adding a charm, to complete the necklace. After the fringe is completed, tie off any remaining threads.

FLOWER GARDEN NECKLACE

I like to make necklaces that are a little asymmetrical and that have a clasp in the front. I think this makes them unique and easier to put on. For a while, all of my designs had a floral theme. This is one of my favorites. The strap is a little tricky to get started and it is time-consuming, but I think it is worth the effort!

Materials

size 12 beading needle

size D Nymo thread

seven 4mm round beads

six 5mm bicone crystals

six drop beads

two 3mm fire polish bead

one 6mm rondelle bead

12 grams size 11 Japanese seed beads for main color

2 grams size 11 Japanese seed beads for accent color

4 grams size 15 Japanese seed beads for main color

3 grams size 15 Japanese seed beads for accent color

2 grams size 8 Japanese seed beads for the fringe

 **THREE STARS**

Rope chain pattern 1

Start with approximately 2yd. (2m) of thread, single thickness with no knot. Pick up two main color size 11 beads and go back through them from the tail end. This will make them sit side by side. Leave a 10"-12" (25cm-30cm) tail; this will be used later for part of the clasp.

Pick up one main color size 11 bead and go through the bead the thread is exiting from on the opposite side. Go through the bead that was just added. There should now be a total of three beads laying side by side.

Rope chain pattern 2

Now the beads need to be turned into a tube shape. To do this, circle stitch the first bead and the last bead together. It will look like a small triangle.

Rope chain pattern 3

The working thread should be coming out of the top of one of the beads. Pick up two main color size 11 beads and go under the second thread over from where the thread is exiting. Go back up the second bead. This will make the two beads sit on top of the original three beads.

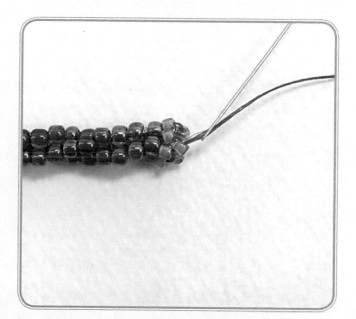

Rope chain pattern 5

The working thread should be coming out of a bead on the end of the rope.

Pick up three size 15 main color beads and go back through the same bead that the thread originally exited from on the same side. This creates a picot on top of the size 11 main color bead of the rope.

Go through the next size 11 main color bead of the rope and repeat two more times. There should be three picots at the end of the rope.

After completing the last picot, go through the first two size 15 main color beads of the first picot. This lines you up to start the next row.

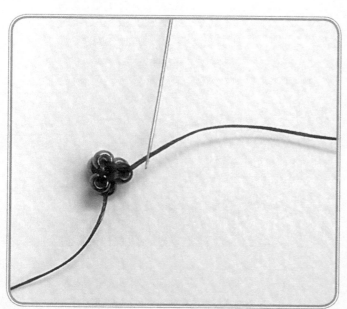

Rope chain pattern 4

Pick up one main color size 11 bead and go under the next thread. Go back up the bead that was just picked up.

Go down through the first bead of this row and come up the next bead. This adds the last thread that connects the triangle together. Three beads should now be connected by three threads.

As you add the rows of beads, the rope will twist. Repeat rope chain pattern 3-4 until the rope is the desired length. A good approximate length is 17" (43cm).

87

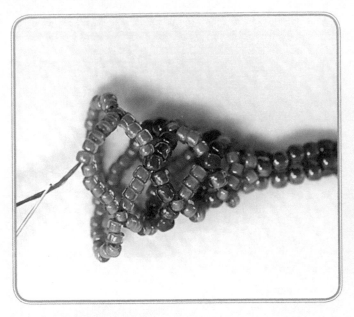

Rope chain pattern 6

Pick up three size 15 main color beads and go through the next center bead of the next picot. Repeat two more times.

Go through the first two beads of the first picot after you create the last picot of this row. This lines you up to start the next row. The remaining rows of netting will be done in the same way. When a row is finished, always go through the beads of the first picot and come out of the center bead before you start the next row.

The bead count below is for the remaining rows of netting.

Row 3: three size 11 main color beads
Row 4: seven size 15 main color beads
Row 5: five size 11 main color beads
Row 6: nine size 15 main color beads
Row 7: eleven size 15 main color beads

Rope chain pattern 7

There are a total of six fringes that hang from the netting. The three shortest fringes hang from the center bead of the last row of netting. The three longest fringes hang from the center bead of the netting from the second-to-last row. The first fringe made is a short fringe.

Follow the bead sequence below for the first short fringe.

1. one size 11 main color bead	*8. three size 15 main color beads*
2. one size 8 bead	*9. one size 11 main color bead*
3. one size 11 main color bead	*10. one size 8 bead*
4. three size 15 main color beads	*11. one size 11 main color bead*
5. one size 11 main color bead	*12. one drop bead*
6. one 5mm Bicone crystal	*13. three size 11 main color beads*
7. one size 11 main color bead	

Rope chain pattern 8

After you make the first short fringe, needle over to the center bead of the previous row and create a long fringe following the bead sequence below. Keep working around the netting, creating fringe alternating between a short fringe and a long fringe.

Follow the bead sequence below for the first long fringe.

1. one size 11 main color bead	*11. one size 11 main color bead*
2. one size 8 bead	*12. three size 15 main color beads*
3. one size 11 main color bead	*13. one size 11 main color bead*
4. one size 8 bead	*14. one size 8 bead*
5. one 4mm round bead	*15. one 4mm round bead*
6. one size 8 bead	*16. one size 8 bead*
7. one size 11 main color bead	*17. one size 15 main color bead*
8. three size 15 main color beads	*18. one drop bead*
9. one size 11 main color bead	*19. three size 11 main color beads*
10. one 5mm bicone crystal	

Rope chain pattern 9

Add the 6mm rondelle bead for the clasp at the netting end of the rope. To do this, weave the working thread so it is coming out of a main color size 11 bead close to the end of the rope before the netting begins.

Pick up one size 11 main color bead, the 6mm rondelle and another size 11 main color bead. Skip the last size 11 main color bead and go back through the 6mm rondelle bead and the next size 11 main color bead.

Go through the size 11 main color bead of the rope that the thread originally exited from on the opposite side. Reinforce.

Rope chain pattern 10

On the other end of the rope, a working thread should be coming out of a size 11 main color bead at the end. Pick up one size 8 bead and then enough size 11 main color beads to fit comfortably around the clasp bead.

Go back down the size 8 bead and go through the size 11 main color bead next to the one that the thread originally exited from. Reinforce.

Flower pattern 1

Start a new working thread with approximately 2½yd. (2.5m) of thread, single thickness with no knot. Pick up one 4mm round bead and six size 11 main color beads. Go back through the 4mm bead from the tail end. Go back through the six size 11 main color beads and the 4mm bead again. Leave a 4"–6" (10cm–15cm) tail.

Pick up six size 11 main color beads and go back through the 4mm bead on the opposite side from where the thread originally exited. Go back through the six beads just added and back through the 4mm bead again.

Go through all the size 11 main color beads. This will pull the beads into a circle around the 4mm bead.

Flower pattern 2

The working thread should now be coming out of a size 11 main color bead. Pick up fourteen size 15 accent beads and one size 11 main color bead. Skip the main color bead and go back through the last size 15 bead that was picked up.

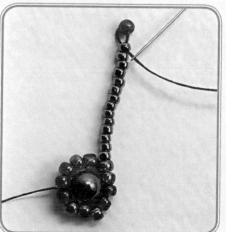

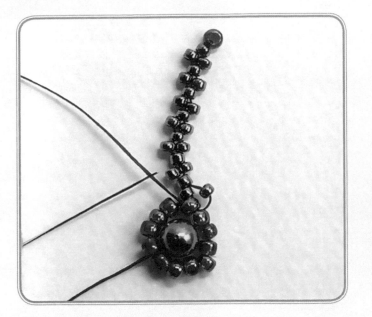

Flower pattern 3

Pick up one size 15 accent bead, skip the next accent bead and go through the next one.

Continue adding beads this way until you get to the last size 15 accent bead. Pick up one size 15 accent bead and go through the size 11 main color bead on the opposite side from where the thread originally exited. This is the first pass of a petal.

Flower pattern 4

Go up through the first size 15 accent bead. Pick up one size 15 accent bead and go through the next accent bead that is sticking out.

Continue until you have gone all the way up the side of the petal. Then needle down to the second-to-last accent bead from the tip main color bead. This turns you around to do the other side of the petal.

Flower pattern 5

Pick up one size 15 accent bead and go down through the next accent bead that sticks out.

Continue until you have gone through the last accent bead. Go through the size 11 main color bead and through the first two accent beads on the side of the petal.

Flower pattern 6

Pick up one size 15 accent bead and go up through the next accent bead that sticks out.

Continue until you get to the last bead that sticks out.

Flower pattern 7

Needle up and over and come down the first bead that sticks out on the other side of the petal.

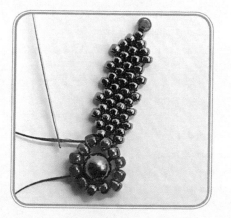

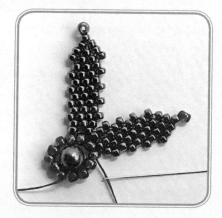

Flower pattern 8

Pick up one size 15 accent bead and go down through the next bead that sticks out.

Repeat until you get to the last bead that sticks out. Then needle through the remaining size 15 beads, the size 11 main color bead and the next size 11 main color bead. This lines the thread up to start the next petal.

Flower pattern 9

The next petal is worked as described in flower pattern 2-8, except it starts with twelve size 15 accent beads instead of fourteen. This will make the petal slightly smaller.

Flower pattern 10

Keep making petals, alternating between making a petal with fourteen beads and a petal with twelve beads.

The finished flower will have six petals of each size for a total of twelve petals. Pull the smaller petals forward so they are on the top of the flower.

Flower pattern 11

To make an eight petal flower, follow the same process as the twelve petal flower, however the center bead will be a 3mm bead and there will be a total of eight size 11 accent beads around the 3mm center bead.

The petals are also smaller in size. The largest petal is made with twelve size 15 main color beads and the smaller petal is made with ten of the size 15 main color beads. Use a size 11 accent bead on the tips of the flowers.

Make two of the eight petal flowers.

Assembly 1

Attach the large twelve petal flower to the rope on the side with the netting, by sewing it close to (but not covering) the netting.

To sew the flower on, weave a working thread so it is coming out of a main color bead on the rope. Go through a bead on the back of the flower, then go through a bead on the rope. Continue sewing the flower to the rope until the flower is secure.

Sew one of the smaller flowers next to the large flower on the netting side of the rope. Sew the other small flower to the loop end of the rope, close to the end so when the necklace is clasped the flowers meet.

Refer to the color photo of the necklace for placement.

PICOT NECKLACE, BRACELET & EARRINGS

The first picot piece I made was an idea for some earrings. It didn't turn out quite like I wanted, and I put it away in my sample box (my shoebox full of little pieces of beadwork that didn't quite work out). About a year later, I pulled the sample out and decided it had potential after all. With a little tweaking it became the earrings. I couldn't just stop at earrings though, so I went on to make the necklace and bracelet.

So, the moral of this story is, save all of those little bits and pieces that don't turn out how you want; put them in a box. Then when you need inspiration, pull out that box. You might be surprised at what good ideas you can get from those pieces that seemed useless before.

TWO STARS ✺ ✺

Necklace Materials

size 12 beading needle

size D Nymo thread

five 6mm round crystals

five 4mm bicone crystals

five drop beads

one 8mm bead

4 grams size 11 Japanese seed beads for main color

8 grams size 15 Japanese seed beads for accent color

Bracelet Materials

size 12 beading needle

size D Nymo thread

six 6mm round crystals

fourteen 4mm bicone crystals

one 8mm bead

5 grams size 11 Japanese seed beads for main color

3 grams size 15 Japanese seed beads for accent color

Earring Materials

size 12 beading needle

size D Nymo thread

two 6mm round crystals

two 4mm bicone crystals

two drop beads

pair of earwires

2 grams size 11 Japanese seed beads for main color

2 grams size 15 Japanese seed beads for accent color

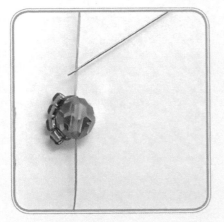

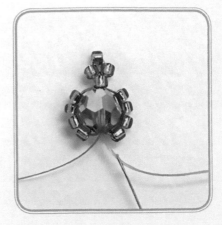

Picot piece pattern 1

Start with approximately 1½yd. (1.5m) of thread, single thickness with no knot. Pick up one 6mm crystal and four size 11 seed beads. Go back through the crystal on the opposite side from where the thread originally exited.

Go through the four seed beads and the crystal again. Leave a 4"–6" (10cm–15cm) tail. The working thread should now be coming out of the 6mm crystal.

Picot piece pattern 2

Pick up four size 11 seed beads and go through the crystal on the opposite side from where the thread originally exited.

Go back through the four seed beads again. Go back through the crystal.

Picot piece pattern 3

The working thread should be coming out of the 6mm crystal. Pick up four size 11 seed beads and go back down the first seed bead you picked up on the same side that the thread exited. Go down through the crystal. This creates a picot on the end of the crystal.

Picot piece pattern 4

The working thread should now be on the other side of the crystal from the picot. Pick up four size 11 seed beads and go back through the first seed bead on the same side that the thread exited.

Go back through the crystal. This creates another picot on the other end of the crystal.

Picot piece pattern 5

Go through the first seed bead of one of the four on the side of the crystal.

Pick up four size 11 seed beads. Go back down the first size 11 seed bead (this creates a picot) and go through the next seed bead along the side of the crystal. This positions the picot in between the beads along the edge of the crystal.

Picot piece pattern 6

Repeat picot piece pattern 5 two more times.

Picot piece pattern 7

Go through the crystal. Repeat picot piece pattern 5–6 on the other side to make three picots on the other side of the crystal to match the first side.

Picot piece pattern 8

Go through the crystal and then weave the thread so it is coming out of the center bead of the picot that is over the hole of the crystal (the top picot).

Pick up six size 15 seed beads. Go back down the third bead you picked up (go through the bead on the same side the thread originally exited). This creates a picot out of the last four beads. Pull this down snug against the first two beads. Pick up two size 15 seed beads and go through the center bead of the next picot on the side of the crystal.

Picot piece pattern 9

Repeat the second half of picot piece pattern 8 two more times.

Picot piece pattern 10

Pick up three size 15 seed beads and four size 11 seed beads. Go back down the first size 11 bead (go through the bead on the same side the thread originally exited). This creates a picot. Make sure that it is snug against the three size 15 beads.

Pick up three more size 15 beads and go through the center bead of the next picot.

Picot piece pattern 11

Pick up eight size 15 seed beads, one 4mm crystal, six size 15 seed beads, one drop bead and six size 15 seed beads. Go back through the 4mm crystal on the opposite side from where the thread originally exited.

Picot piece pattern 12

Pick up eight size 15 seed beads and go back through the picot bead the thread originally exited from on the opposite side. Repeat the picots made on this side in a mirror image on the other side. Tie off the tail thread but leave the working thread attached.

Repeat picot piece pattern 1–12 to create four picot pieces for a total of five for the necklace.

Assembly 1

You will assemble the picot pieces from left to right. Pick up one picot piece and weave its working thread so it comes out of the center bead of the picot using a circle stitch (see *Circle Stitch* on page 13) to attach the two center picot beads together (refer to the photo for placement). Reinforce.

Assembly 2

Continue connecting the picot pieces together using circle stitches. The picot-to-picot connection points vary between each piece, so refer to the photo for the proper connections. Attach the pieces from left to right.

Assembly 3

Weave a working thread so it is coming out of the center bead of the picot that is above the first connection. It needs to be going through the center bead of the picot going down toward the beadwork. Pick up nine size 15 beads and go through the center bead of the picot on the next piece above the original connection.

Pick up eleven size 15 beads and go back through the picot bead the thread originally exited from on the opposite side. This makes an oval of beads between the picots above the original connection. The nine beads must be on the bottom of the oval and the eleven beads must be on the top of the oval.

Assembly 4

Go through the first five size 15 beads of the nine that were added in step 15. Pick up three size 15 beads and go back through the fifth bead on the opposite side. This creates a picot on top of the fifth bead.

Weave through the last four beads of the nine beads and go through the picot bead and the first four size 15 beads of the eleven beads that were added in assembly 3. Pick up three size 15 beads and go back through the fourth bead on the opposite side. This creates another picot.

Weave through the size 15 beads and come out the eighth bead of the eleven beads and create another picot with size 15 beads. Weave through the remaining three size 15 beads.

Assembly 5

Make three more ovals with picots as described in assembly 3-4. Refer to the photo for proper placement.

Tie off any working threads except for the two threads that are closest to the end picot pieces.

Chain pattern 1

Weave a working thread (you need approximately 24" [61cm] of thread) so it is coming out of the center bead of the second picot above the size 11 bead picot.

Pick up seven size 15 beads, one size 11 bead and seven more size 15 beads. Go back through the picot bead the thread originally exited from on the opposite side.

Chain pattern 2

Go through the first four size 15 beads of the seven. Pick up three size 15 beads and go back through the size 15 bead the thread exited from on the opposite side. This creates a picot on top of the fourth size 15 bead.

97

Chain pattern 3

Weave over to the fourth bead of the other group of seven beads and repeat chain pattern 2 to make a picot. There should be a picot on each side of the circle.

Chain pattern 4

Weave the thread so it is coming out of the size 11 bead of the circle. Pick up seven size 15 beads, one size 11 bead and seven size 15 beads. Go back through the size 11 bead on the opposite side from where the thread originally exited. Repeat chain pattern 2–3 to make picots.

Repeat chain pattern 4, making circles with picots until the strap is the desired length. A good average length has seventeen circles.

Chain pattern 5

To add the 8mm clasp bead, the thread should be coming out of the size 11 bead of the last circle. Pick up seven size 15 beads, one size 11 bead, the 8mm bead and three size 11 beads. Skip the last three size 11 beads and go back through the 8mm bead and the size 11 bead.

Pick up seven more size 15 beads and go through the size 11 bead that the thread originally exited from on the opposite side. Reinforce.

Chain pattern 6

Repeat chain pattern 1–5 on the other side of your piece for the second strap section. However, on this end, add a loop of size 15 beads that fits comfortably but snugly around the 8mm bead. Reinforce.

Tie off any remaining threads.

BRACELET

Picot bracelet pattern 1

Follow picot piece pattern 1–8 from the Picot Necklace. Repeat pattern 8 seven more times so you end up with eight picots around this piece.

Repeat this step to make five or six more of the picot pieces. The number you need to make will depend on how long you want the bracelet. Five pieces makes a bracelet that is approximately 7½" (18cm) long.

Bracelet assembly 1

Tie off any tail threads on the picot pieces but leave the working threads.

Weave a working thread so it is coming out of the center bead of one of the picots that is closest to the hole of the 6mm crystal. Pick up one size 11 bead, one 4mm crystal and one size 11 bead. Go through the center picot bead of the corresponding picot of another picot piece.

Bracelet assembly 2

Pick up one more size 11 bead and go back through the 4mm crystal.

Pick up one size 11 bead and go through the picot bead the thread originally exited from on the opposite side.

Bracelet assembly 3

Weave the thread down to the next picot that is on the other side of the hole of the 6mm crystal and repeat bracelet assembly 1–2.

Repeat bracelet assembly 1–3 until all the picot pieces are connected.

Bracelet assembly 4

Choose one end of the connected pieces to add the clasp. Weave a working thread so it is coming out of the center bead of the picot that is closest to the hole of the 6mm crystal.

Pick up one size 11 bead, one of the 4mm crystals, two size 11 beads, the 8mm bead and three size 11 beads. Skip the last three size 11 beads and go back down the 8mm bead and the next size 11 bead.

Pick up one size 11 bead, one 4mm crystal and one size 11 bead. Go through the center bead of the picot next to the one the thread originally came out of. Reinforce.

Bracelet assembly 5

On the other end of the bracelet, repeat bracelet assembly 4, but add a loop of size 11 beads that fits comfortably but snugly around the 8mm bead. Reinforce.

Tie off any remaining threads.

EARRINGS

Earring pattern 1

Follow picot piece pattern 1–7 from the Picot Necklace. Go through the crystal and weave the thread so it is coming out of the center bead of the picot that is over the hole of the crystal (the top picot).

Pick up twelve size 15 seed beads and an earwire. Go back through the center bead of the picot on the opposite side that the thread exited from. Reinforce.

Earring pattern 2

Pick up six size 15 seed beads and go back down the third bead (go through the bead on the same side the thread originally exited from). This creates a picot out of the last four beads. Be sure to pull this snug against the first two beads.

Pick up two size 15 seed beads and go through the center bead of the next picot on the side of the crystal.

Earring pattern 3

Repeat earring pattern 2 two more times.

Earring pattern 4

Pick up three size 15 seed beads and four size 11 seed beads. Go back down the first size 11 seed bead (go through the bead on the same side the thread originally exited). This creates a picot. Make sure that it is snug against the three size 15 beads.

Pick up three size 15 seed beads and go through the center bead of the next picot.

Earring pattern 5

Pick up eight size 15 seed beads, one 4mm crystal, six size 15 seed beads, one drop bead and six size 15 seed beads. Go back through the 4mm crystal on the opposite side from where the thread originally exited.

Earring pattern 6

Pick up eight size 15 seed beads and go back through the picot bead the thread originally exited from on the opposite side.

Repeat earring pattern 2–6 to add picots in a mirror image on the other side of the earring. Weave in and tie off the working and tail threads.

Repeat earring pattern 1–6 for the other earring.

CRYSTAL AND PICOT NECKLACE

At a bead show, I had purchased an entire box of vintage crystals and decided I needed to do something with them besides admire them in my personal stash (something I do all too often). This necklace showcases the vintage bead within a vintage-inspired pattern. If you don't have access to any vintage crystals, any 12mm bead will work. A flat coin shape works the best, but a round bead will also work.

Materials

size 12 beading needle

size D Nymo thread

one 12mm crystal or bead

eleven 4mm bicone crystals

three 6mm round or bicone crystals

three drop beads

one 8mm fire polish bead

8 grams size 11 Japanese seed beads for main color

8 grams size 11 Japanese seed beads for accent color

TWO STARS

Focal crystal pattern 1

Start with approximately 2yd. (2m) of thread, single thickness with no knot. Pick up the 12mm crystal and then pick up 15 main color beads. Go back through all the beads again from the tail end. Leave a 4"-6" (10cm-15cm) tail. Go back through the 12mm crystal.

Focal crystal pattern 2

Pick up fifteen main color beads and go through the 12mm crystal on the opposite side from where the thread originally exited.

Go back through the fifteen main color beads that were just added.

Go through all thirty main color beads and pull the thread snug.

Focal crystal pattern 3

The working thread should now be coming out a main color bead. Pick up two main color beads, one accent bead and two main color beads. Skip over two beads of the circle and go through the third bead.

Repeat this step until you have gone all the way around the original circle. After completing the last stitch, go up through the first two main color beads and the first accent bead that were picked up in this row. This completes the row and lines the thread up for the next row.

Focal crystal pattern 4

The working thread should be coming out of an accent bead. Pick up three main color beads, one accent bead and three more main color beads. Go through the next accent bead of the previous row.

Focal crystal pattern 5

Pick up one main color bead, one 4mm crystal and one main color bead. Go through the next accent bead of the previous row.

Focal crystal pattern 6

Repeat focal crystal pattern 4-5 until you have gone all the way around the circle.

After completing the last stitch, weave up to the first accent bead of this row.

Chain pattern 1

The working thread should now be coming out of an accent bead from the last row. Pick up three main color beads, one accent bead and three main color beads. Go back through the accent bead the thread is exiting from on the opposite side and also go through the first two main color beads. This makes a small circle of beads.

Chain pattern 2

Pick up three accent beads and go back through the main color bead that the thread is coming out of on the opposite side from where it originally exited. This creates a picot on the circle.

Weave over to the middle main color bead on the other side of the circle. Follow this step to create a picot on this side of the circle.

Chain pattern 3

Weave the working thread so it is coming out of the accent bead at the top of the circle.

Chain pattern 4

Repeat chain pattern 1–3 until you have the strap the desired length. An average length is about 8¹/₂" (22cm) including the closure.

After reaching the desired length, come out of the accent bead at the top of the last circle. Pick up three main color beads, one accent bead, the 8mm bead and three accent beads. Skip the last three accent beads and go back through the 8mm bead and the next accent bead.

Pick up three main color beads and go through the accent bead of the strap on the opposite side from where the thread originally exited. Reinforce.

Chain pattern 5

Weave a working thread (you need approximately 24" [61cm] of thread) so it is coming out of the accent bead that is the third point over from where the first side of the strap is attached.

Chain pattern 6

Repeat chain pattern 1–4 until you have the desired length on this side of the piece; instead of adding the closure bead, you will add a looped end.

To do this, come out the end accent bead and pick up enough beads to fit snugly but comfortably over the 8mm bead. Go through the accent bead of the strap on the opposite side. Reinforce.

Fringe pattern 1

Weave a working thread so it is coming out of the accent bead of the picot below the strap (the one without the 4mm crystal).

Pick up three main color beads, one accent bead and three main color beads. Go through the accent bead your thread is exiting from on the opposite side.

Go back through the first two main color beads. Pick up three accent beads and go back through the main color bead your thread is coming out of on the opposite side. This creates a picot.

Fringe pattern 2

Weave up to the top accent bead and create another picot with three more accent beads.

Fringe pattern 3

Weave over to the second main color bead and create one more picot with three accent beads.

Fringe pattern 4

Weave around so the working thread is coming out of the center bead of the bottom picot. Pick up the following bead sequence:

1. *three main beads*
2. *one accent bead*
3. *one 4mm crystal*
4. *one accent bead*
5. *one 6mm crystal*
6. *one accent bead*
7. *one 4mm crystal*
8. *one accent bead*
9. *four main beads*
10. *one accent bead*
11. *one drop bead*
12. *one accent bead*
13. *four main beads*

Go back up the accent bead below the last 4mm bead that was added and go back up to the first accent bead picked up. Pick up three main color beads and go through the accent picot bead the thread originally exited from on the opposite side. This completes a fringe.

Fringe pattern 5

Weave over to the next point that does not have a 4mm crystal and repeat fringe pattern 1–4

Fringe pattern 6

Weave over to the last point that doesn't have a 4mm crystal and repeat fringe pattern 1–4. There should now be three fringes.

Fringe pattern 7

Weave the working thread so it is coming out of the center bead of the center picot on one of the side fringes.

Pick up three main color beads, one accent bead and three main color beads. Go back through the accent bead your thread exited from on the opposite side and also go through the first three main color beads and the accent bead. This creates a circle. Repeat two more times.

Fringe pattern 8

Pick up three accent beads and go through the accent bead your thread is coming out of on the opposite side. This creates a picot at the end of the three circle chain.

Using a circle stitch (see *Circle Stitch* on page 13), attach the center bead of the picot to the center bead of the third picot on the strap (refer to the picture for clarification).

Repeat fringe pattern 7–8 on the other side of the necklace. Tie off any remaining threads.

STARFLOWER NECKLACE

This is great project for a spring day. Make one to go with all of your spring outfits! The flower could also be made into a pin by simply omitting the strap and adding a pinback finding to the back of the flower.

Materials

size 12 beading needle

size D Nymo thread

ten 4mm fire polish beads

nine 4mm bicone crystals

nine drop beads

two 8mm fire polish beads

11 grams size 11 Japanese seed beads for main color

3 grams size 11 Japanese seed beads for accent color

4 grams size 11 Japanese seed beads for a flower tip color

7 grams size 11 Japanese seed beads for a strap accent color

4 grams size 11 Japanese seed beads for fringe

ONE STAR

Flower pendant pattern 1

Start with approximately 2½yd. (2.5m) of thread, single thickness with no knot. Pick up one 8mm bead and ten main color seed beads. Go back through all the beads from the tail end. Go back through the 8mm bead. Leave a 4"-6" (10cm-15cm) tail.

Flower pendant pattern 2

Pick up ten main color beads and go back through the 8mm bead on the opposite side from where the thread originally exited.

Go through all twenty of the main color beads. This will make a circle of main color beads around the 8mm center bead.

Flower pendant pattern 3

The working thread should now be coming out of one of the main color beads.

Pick up six accent seed beads and one main color bead. Skip the main color bead and go back through the sixth accent bead.

Flower pendant pattern 4

Pick up five accent beads and go through the second bead over from where the thread is exiting the original circle of beads. Do not count the bead the thread is coming out of.

This creates a small triangle (a petal) with one bead of the original circle in the middle.

Flower pendant pattern 5

Repeat pendant pattern 3-4 until you have a total of ten triangles. This completes the first layer of petals.

Flower pendant pattern 6

The second layer of petals is offset slightly from the first layer.

Weave through the next bead of the original circle of main color beads. (It is the bead that is in the center of the triangle of the first layer of petals.) Pick up ten main color beads and one flower tip bead.

Skip the flower tip bead and go back through the tenth main color bead.

Flower pendant pattern 7

Pick up nine main color beads, skip the next bead of the original ring of main color beads and go through the next bead (it will be the second bead over from where the thread is exiting from the original ring of beads). This creates a slightly larger triangle or petal than the triangles of the first layer.

Flower pendant pattern 8

Repeat flower pendant pattern 6-7 until there are ten triangles.

This layer creates the bottom layer of the flower; the shorter layer is the top layer.

Flower pendant pattern 9

Weave the working thread so it is coming out of the 8mm bead on the back of the flower.

Pick up ten main color beads and go back through the 8mm bead on the opposite side from where the thread originally exited.

Go through the first main color bead.

Flower pendant pattern 10

The fringe will hang from the group of beads added in flower pendant pattern 9. There are a total of nine fringes and they hang between the ten beads.

The first follows this pattern:

1. six size 11 fringe beads

2. one size 11 flower tip bead

3. one 4mm fire polish bead

4. one size 11 flower tip bead

5. three size 11 fringe beads

6. one size 11 flower tip bead

7. one 4mm bicone crystal

8. one size 11 flower tip bead

9. one drop bead

10. three size 11 fringe beads

For the next fringes, increase by two fringe beads at the top of the fringe for each subsequent fringe until you get to the center fringe (the fifth fringe).

The center fringe has a total of fourteen fringe beads at the top of the fringe. There is also an extra 4mm fire polish bead toward the end of the fringe (refer to the photo for the other bead placement of the fringe).

After the center fringe, decrease by two fringe beads at the top of each fringe, creating a mirror image of the fringe you have already added.

Flower pendant pattern 11

Weave the working thread so it is coming out of the 8mm bead on the back side of the flower.

Pick up ten main color beads. Go back through the 8mm bead on the opposite side from where the thread originally exited.

Go back through this one more time to reinforce it.

Chain pattern 1

The strap is worked separately from the pendant in two pieces and is attached after it is completed.

Start a new thread approximately 2yd. (2m), single thickness with no knot. Pick up one main color bead, one strap accent bead and one main color bead. Tie the tail and working thread into a knot.

This will make a small triangle. Leave an 8"–10" (20cm–25cm) tail.

Chain pattern 2

Pick up one main color bead, one strap accent bead and one main color bead. Go back up one of the original main color beads.

Chain pattern 3

Pick up one strap accent bead and one main color bead. Go down the main color bead that is below the one the thread is exiting from.

Chain pattern 4

Pick up one strap accent bead and one main color bead. Go up the main color bead that is above the one the thread is exiting from.

Repeat chain pattern 3-4 until this half of the strap is the desired length. A good approximate length is 7" (18cm) without the clasp.

Chain pattern 5

The working thread should be coming out of one of the main color beads at the end of the strap.

Pick up four main color beads, an 8mm bead and three strap accent beads. Skip the three strap accent beads and go back through the 8mm bead and the next main color bead.

Pick up three main color beads and go through the main color bead at the end of the strap that is next to the one that the thread originally exited from. Reinforce.

Chain pattern 6

Repeat chain pattern 1-4 to make the second strap piece the same size as the first one.

Weave the working thread so it is coming out of one of the main color beads at the end of the strap. Pick up enough main color beads to fit comfortably but snugly around the 8mm bead. Go through the main color bead next to the one that the thread originally exited from. Reinforce.

Assembly 1

Put a needle on the tail thread at the end of one of the strap pieces. Weave the thread so it is coming out of a main color bead going away from the strap.

Go through the first and second bead of the ten beads you added to the 8mm center bead in flower pendant pattern 11. Go through the main color bead of the strap that is next to the bead that the thread originally exited from. This will make a circle stitch (see *Circle Stitch* on page 13). Reinforce.

Repeat this step with the other strap piece on the ninth and tenth beads of the ten beads that were added to the 8mm center bead in flower pendant pattern 11. Reinforce. Tie off any remaining threads.

tip

After the necklace is finished, you may want to stiffen the flower a little. Use a soft brush and a clear floor polish. Brush a light coat on the petals of the flower. Let this dry overnight. You can also use clear fingernail polish to help stiffen the petals.

CHAIN LARIAT

This lariat is a versatile piece of jewelry. It can be worn with the ring up against the neck for a funky choker look; the chain can be wrapped several times around the ring, adding some texture and drama; or it can be worn more loosely to suit a freer mood. Consider making the chain longer to create a stunning, delicate belt.

Materials

size 12 beading needle

size D Nymo thread

fifteen assorted crystals and beads from 4mm to 6mm in size

two glass drop beads

one sterling or pewter charm

one medium sterling spacer bead with fairly large hole

one small sterling bead cap

one sterling ring

16 grams size 11 Japanese seed beads for main color

2 grams size 11 Japanese seed beads for accent color

ONE STAR

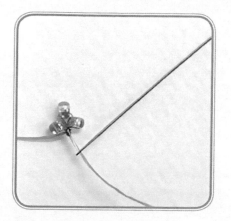

Chain pattern 1

Start with approximately 2yd. (2m) of thread, single thickness with no knot. Pick up three main color beads and tie them into a triangle. Leave an 8"–10" (20cm–25cm) tail, which is used later to sew the ring to the end of the chain.

Chain pattern 2

Pick up six main color beads and go back through two beads of the original three beads that are tied into a triangle. Pull snug.

Chain pattern 3

Pick up three main color beads and go back through the fifth and fourth bead from the previous six beads that were picked up. This is done in a zigzag thread path. The thread snakes back and forth. Pull snug.

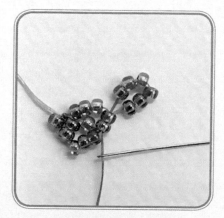

Chain pattern 4

Pick up six main color beads and go back through the fourth and fifth beads (the beads you just came out of) in the opposite direction. Pull snug.

Chain pattern 5

Pick up three main color beads and go through the fifth and fourth bead from the previous six beads that were picked up. Pull snug.

Chain pattern 6

Pick up six main color beads and go back through the fourth and fifth bead (the beads you just came out of) in the opposite direction. Pull snug.

Repeat chain pattern 5–6 until the chain is the desired length. A good average length is 24" (61cm) without the fringe.

Chain pattern 7

If the working thread is long enough, it can be used to add the fringe. Otherwise, tie off the old working thread and start a new one approximately 2yd. (2m) of thread, single thickness with no knot.

Weave the working thread so it is coming out of a bead on the end of the chain. Pick up the medium spacer bead and the small bead cap.

Pick up three main color beads and then pick up an assortment of crystals and main color and accent beads. The fringe can be as long or as short as you prefer.

After you have the fringe beads picked up, skip the end drop bead and go back up the remaining beads including the bead cap and spacer bead. Turn around in the beads at the end of the chain and come back down through the spacer bead and the bead cap.

Repeat this step until you have a total of three fringes.

Assembly 1

On the other end of the chain, use the tail left in chain pattern 1 to add the sterling ring. The thread should be coming out of a bead at the end of the chain.

Go through the ring with the thread and then fold the end of the chain over and tack it to itself by going through the beads of the chain and the beads at the end of the chain. There is no right or wrong way to do this; just make it look as neat as possible. Tie off any remaining threads.

WAVY ROSETTE NECKLACE

This necklace is easily adjustable to fit your own personal tastes. Make it longer or shorter by adjusting the number of wavy rosettes. A long version could be worn doubled for another style option.

Materials

size 12 beading needle

size D Nymo thread

two-hundred-twenty 4mm fire polish beads for accent color

30 grams size 11 Japanese seed beads for main color

3 grams size 8 Japanese seed beads for accent color

TWO STARS ✦ ✦

Wavy rosette pattern 1

Start with approximately 1yd. (1m) of thread, single thickness with no knot. Pick up nine size 11 beads. Go back through all nine beads from the tail end. This will make a circle. Leave a 4"–6" (10cm–15cm) tail.

To close the circle more completely, also go through the next five beads.

Wavy rosette pattern 2

Pick up one 4mm bead and go through the bead that the tail is coming out of. Tie the working thread and the tail thread into a knot. This will keep the circle of beads from slipping open.

Wavy rosette pattern 3

Pick up one size 11 bead and go back through the size 11 bead the working thread is coming out of on the opposite side from where the thread exited. Go through the next size 11 bead. The bead just added should be sitting on top of the bead below it of the original circle. Repeat until you have added nine size 11 beads.

Wavy rosette pattern 4

Weave up to one of the top beads of the row just added. Pick up one size 11 bead and go back through the bead the thread is exiting from on the opposite side. This bead will sit on top of the bead from the last row.

Wavy rosette pattern 5

Pick up one size 11 bead and go through the next bead over (it will be a bead from the last row). This bead will sit in between the beads of the last row.

Wavy rosette pattern 6

Repeat wavy rosette pattern 4–5 until you have gone all the way around the circle. Nine beads will sit on top of the previous row, and nine beads will sit in between the beads.

Wavy rosette pattern 7

Now weave the working thread so it is coming out of one of the top beads that is sticking out. Pick up one 4mm bead and go through the next bead that is sticking out.

Continue around the row until nine 4mm beads are added between the main color beads that stick out.

The last 4mm bead may need to be squeezed into place. At this point, the rosette may start to ruffle a little bit.

Wavy rosette pattern 8

The working thread should be coming out of a 4mm bead. Pick up three size 11 beads and go through the next 4mm bead. This creates a picot between the 4mm beads.

Repeat this step all the way around the rosette. There should be nine picots. The rosette will become even more wavy at this point. Tie off the tail thread on the rosette but leave the working thread.

Repeat wavy rosette pattern 1–8 to make nineteen more rosettes, for a total of twenty rosettes for the necklace.

Assembly 1

To attach the rosettes, weave a thread so it is coming out of the middle bead of a picot. Pick up three size 11 beads, one size 8 bead, one size 11 bead, one 4mm bead, one size 11 bead, one size 8 bead and three size 11 beads.

Go through the center bead of a picot on another rosette. Go back through the beads just picked up and also go through the picot bead the thread exited from on the opposite side from where the thread originally exited. Reinforce.

When the next rosette is added, attach it at the fourth picot. There should be three picots on one side and four picots on the other side of the connection.

Repeat this step until all twenty rosettes are connected. Tie off any remaining threads.

TIARA NECKLACE, BRACELET & EARRINGS

This necklace can be done in any color combination, but the cream seed beads and pearls make it especially fitting for a bride to wear on her special day.

I didn't initially design the *Tiara Bracelet* when I designed the *Tiara Necklace*. At one point, I thought it would be nice to have a complete set, so I designed the bracelet and earrings to go with the necklace—I think it was a nice afterthought!

TWO STARS ✦ ✦

Necklace Materials

size 12 beading needle

size D Nymo thread

sixty-six 4mm round beads

eight drop beads

one 8mm bead

8 grams size 11 Japanese seed beads for main color

3 grams size 11 Japanese seed beads for accent color

Bracelet Materials

size 12 beading needle

size D Nymo thread

sixty-nine 4mm round beads

one 8mm bead

8 grams size 11 Japanese seed beads for main color

3 grams size 11 Japanese seed beads for accent color

Earring Materials

size 12 beading needle

size D Nymo thread

eighteen 4mm round beads

two drop beads

pair of earwires

4 grams size 11 Japanese seed beads for main color

1 gram size 11 Japanese seed beads for accent color

119

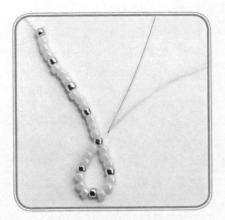

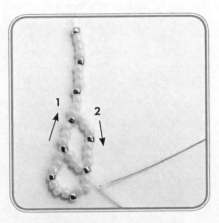

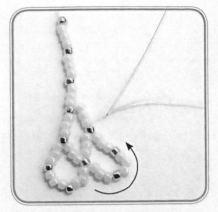

Large triangle pattern 1

Start with approximately 1¹/₂yd. (1.5m) of thread, single thickness with no knot. Pick up one accent bead and turn it into a stopper bead by going back through it from the tail end.

Pick up three main color beads and another accent bead. Repeat until there are a total of eight accent beads and eight groups of main color beads.

Go through the fifth accent bead you picked up in the direction of the tail. Leave a 4"-6" (10cm-15cm) tail.

Large triangle pattern 2

Then weave up through the next three main color beads and the next accent bead (1).

Pick up three main color beads, one accent bead and three main color beads. Skip over an accent bead and go back down through the next accent bead (2).

Large triangle pattern 3

Pick up three main color beads, one accent bead, three main color beads, one accent bead and three main color beads. Go up through the accent bead you picked up in pattern 2.

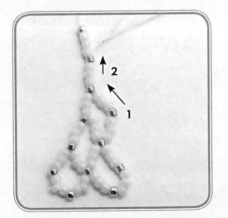

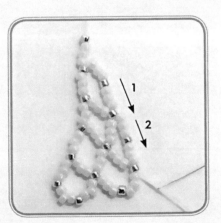

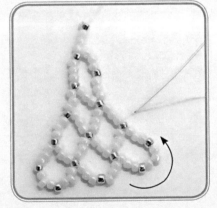

Large triangle pattern 4

Pick up three main color beads, one accent bead and three main color beads. Go up through the third accent bead of pattern 1 (1).

Go up through the next three main color beads and the next accent bead (2).

Large triangle pattern 5

Pick up three main color beads, one accent bead and then three more main color beads. Go down through the the accent bead added in pattern 4 (1).

Pick up three main color beads, one accent bead and three main color beads and go down through the next accent bead that sticks out (2).

Large triangle pattern 6

Pick up three main color beads, one accent bead, three main color beads, one more accent bead and three main color beads. Go up through the last accent bead added in pattern 5.

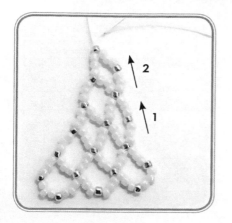

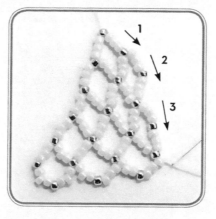

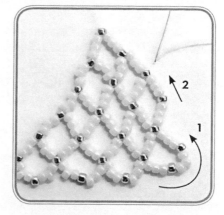

Large triangle pattern 7

Pick up three main color beads, one accent bead and then three more main color beads. Go up through the accent bead that sticks out (1).

Pick up three main color beads, one accent bead and three main color beads. Go through the tip accent bead (2).

Large triangle pattern 8

Weave back down next three main color beads and the next accent bead (1).

Pick up three main color beads, one accent bead and three main color beads. Go down through the next accent bead that sticks out (2).

Pick up three main color beads, one accent bead and three main color beads. Go back down the next accent bead that sticks out (3).

Large triangle pattern 9

Pick up three main color beads, one accent bead, three main color beads, one accent bead and three more main color beads. Go up through the accent bead of the last group of beads that were just picked up (1).

Pick up three main color beads, one accent bead and three more main color beads. Go up through the next accent bead that sticks out (2).

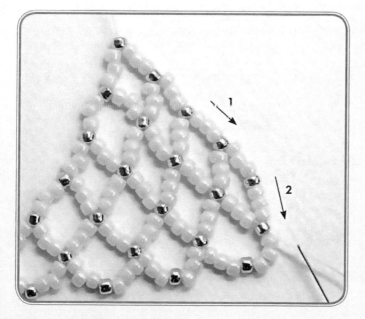

Large triangle pattern 10

Weave down the last three main color beads and the accent bead that was just added (1). Pick up three main color beads, one accent bead and three main color beads. Go down through the next accent bead that sticks out (2).

Large triangle pattern 11

Pick up three main color beads, one accent bead, three main color beads, one accent bead and three more main color beads. Go up through the accent bead picked up in pattern 10. This completes the large triangle.

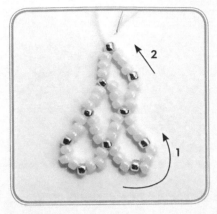

Small triangle pattern 1

Start a new thread, approximately 1yd. (1m) long, single thickness with no knot. Pick up one accent bead and turn it into a stopper bead by going back through it from the tail end. Leave a 4"-6" (10cm-15cm) tail.

Pick up three main color beads and another accent bead until there are a total of six accent beads and six groups of main color beads. Weave back up the third accent bead. Weave up through the next set of main color beads and the next accent bead.

Small triangle pattern 2

Pick up three main color beads, one accent bead and three main color beads. Go down through the accent bead that sticks out.

Small triangle pattern 3

Pick up three main color beads, one accent bead, three main color beads, one accent bead and three main color beads. Weave up through the accent bead that was added in small triangle pattern 2 (1).

Pick up three main color beads, one accent bead and three more main color beads and go through the tip accent bead (2).

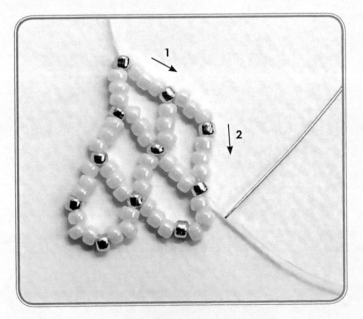

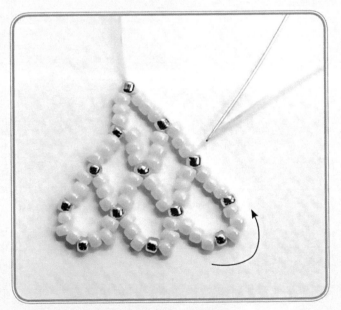

Small triangle pattern 4

Weave down the last three main color beads and the accent bead from pattern 3 (1). Pick up three main color beads, one accent bead and three main color beads. Go down through the accent bead that sticks out (2).

Small triangle pattern 5

Pick up three main color beads, one accent bead, three main color beads, one accent bead and three main color beads. Go up through the accent bead you added in pattern 4. This completes a small triangle.

Repeat small triangle pattern 1-5 to make one more small triangle. There are two small triangles on the necklace.

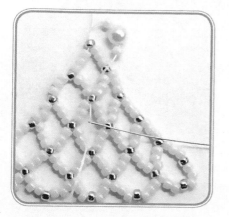 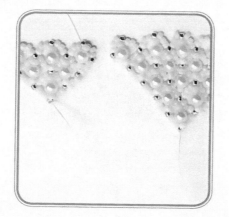 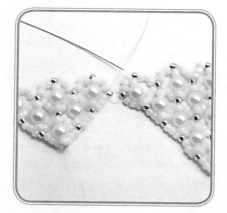

Embellishment 1

After the three triangles are completed, the 4mm beads are added to them.

Start with the large triangle. Weave the working thread up to the tip of the triangle and come out of the accent bead. Pick up one main color bead, one 4mm bead and one main color bead. Go through the accent bead that is in a vertical line below the tip accent bead.

Embellishment 2

Pick up one main color bead, one 4mm bead and one more main color bead. Go down through the next accent bead in a vertical line.

Keep adding the 4mm beads to the open spaces of the netting in this way. They should all cross the netting in a vertical path. Work one half of the triangle and then the other. Weave the thread around the netting as needed.

Add the 4mm beads to the two smaller triangles in the same way.

Assembly 1

Weave the working thread from a small triangle up to the accent bead on the side of the wide end of the triangle. Come out of the accent bead. Using the circle stitch (see *Circle Stitch* on page 13), attach the small triangle to the large triangle at the side accent bead of the wide end of the large triangle. Reinforce.

Repeat this step to attach the remaining small triangle to the other side of the large triangle.

Chain pattern 1

For the chain, weave a working thread so it is coming out of the side accent bead on the wide end of the small triangle.

Pick up one main color bead, one drop bead and one more main color bead. Pick up one 4mm bead, six main color beads and repeat this sequence of a 4mm bead and six main color beads until the chain is the desired length. Approximately 5½" (14cm) is a good length before adding the clasp.

Pick up the 8mm bead and three main color beads. Skip the last three main color beads and go back through the 8mm bead and the next main color bead. Pick up four main color beads and go through the main color bead before the next 4mm bead. Go through the 4mm bead and the next main color bead.

Pick up four main color beads and continue down the strap in this way. When you get to the last bead of the chain, weave the working thread in and tie it off.

Repeat this step on the other small triangle for the other half of the chain. On this end, make a loop of main color beads that fits comfortably but snugly over the 8mm bead.

Flower drop pattern 1

Start a new thread, approximately 1yd. (1m) long, single thickness with no knot. Pick up one main color bead and turn it into a stopper bead by going back through it from the tail end. Leave a 4"–6" (10cm–15cm) tail.

Pick up one 4mm bead and eight main color beads. Go back through the first main color bead. Go through the 4mm bead and the stopper bead. This creates the first petal of the flower drop.

Flower drop pattern 2

Skip the stopper bead and go back through the 4mm bead. Pick up eight main color beads and go back through the first main color bead. Go through the 4mm bead and the stopper bead again.

Repeat two more times for a total of four petals.

Flower drop pattern 3

Skip the stopper bead and go back down the 4mm bead. Pick up two main color beads, a drop bead and three main color beads. Skip the three main color beads and go back up the drop bead, the first two main color beads, the 4mm bead and the stopper bead. This completes the flower drop.

Assembly 2

Repeat flower drop pattern 1–3 four more times to create a total of five flower drops. One drop will be longer than the others by adding two drop beads; this will be the center drop of the necklace.

To attach the flower drops to the triangles, use the working thread from the drops and attach the drop using a circle stitch (see *Circle Stitch* on page 13).

Two drops go on the tip accent beads of the small triangles. Two drops go on the third accent bead up from the tip accent bead of the large triangle. The largest drop goes on the tip accent bead of the large triangle.

BRACELET

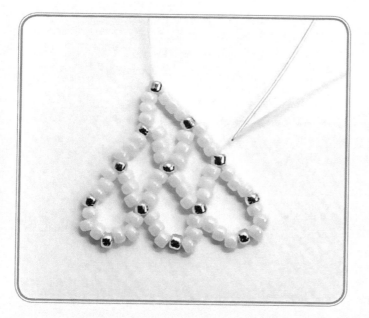

Bracelet pattern 1

To begin the bracelet, follow small triangle pattern 1–5 of the Tiara Necklace (page 122) to make one small triangle.

Bracelet pattern 2

Weave the working thread up to the tip of the triangle and come out of the accent bead. Pick up one main color bead, one 4mm bead and one main color bead. Go through the accent bead that is in a vertical line below the tip accent bead.

Pick up one main color bead, one 4mm bead and one main color bead. Go down through the next accent bead in a vertical line.

Bracelet pattern 3

Repeat bracelet pattern 2 to fill in the netting spaces with 4mm beads. They should all cross the netting in a vertical path. Work one half of the triangle and then the other half. Weave the working thread around the netting as needed and add the 4mm beads in each circle of the netting. Tie off the tail thread and leave the working thread on the triangles.

Repeat bracelet pattern 1–3 until you have a total of six or eight triangles. The number of triangles needed will depend on the length of the bracelet. Six triangles makes a bracelet that is approximately 7" (18cm), and eight triangles make a bracelet that is approximately 8¹/₂" (22cm).

Bracelet assembly 1

Weave a working thread so it is coming out of one of the end accent beads on the wide side of the triangle, working toward the beadwork.

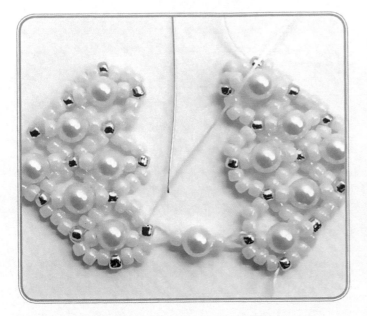

Bracelet assembly 2

Pick up one main color bead, one 4mm bead and one main color bead. Go through the accent bead of another triangle. Us a circle stitch to connect the two pieces. Go back through the main color bead, the 4mm bead and the first main color. Go through the accent bead the thread originally exited from on the opposite side.

Bracelet assembly 3

Weave to the next accent bead that sticks out and repeat bracelet assembly 2. Then weave up to the next accent bead that sticks out and repeat one more time.

Bracelet assembly 4

Weave the thread so it is coming out of the second accent bead on the side of the triangle. Pick up six main color beads, one accent bead, one 4mm bead, one accent bead and six more main color beads. Go through the second accent bead of another triangle.

Go back through the beads that you just picked up and circle back through the accent bead you originally exited from.

Bracelet assembly 5

Weave up to the center accent bead. Pick up one main color bead, one 4mm bead and one more main color bead. Go through the accent bead of the other triangle and go back through the beads just picked up. Go back through the accent bead the thread originally exited from.

Weave up to the second accent bead and repeat bracelet assembly 4.

Repeat bracelet assembly 1–5 until all the triangles are connected.

Closure 1

After connecting all the triangles, weave the working thread so it is coming out the accent bead next to the tip accent bead of the last triangle. Pick up eight main color beads, one accent bead, the 8mm bead and three accent beads. Skip the three accent beads and go back through the 8mm bead and the first accent bead.

Pick up eight more main color beads and go through the accent bead on the other side of the tip accent bead. Reinforce.

Closure 2

On the other end of the bracelet, weave a working thread so it is coming out of the accent bead next to the tip accent bead. Pick up eight main color beads, one accent bead and then enough main color beads to fit comfortably around the 8mm bead. Go back through the accent bead and pick up eight more main color beads.

Go through the other accent bead next to the tip accent bead. Reinforce.

EARRINGS

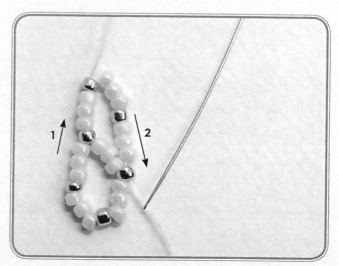

Earring pattern 1

Start with approximately 1yd. (1m) of thread, single thickness with no knot. Pick up one accent bead and turn it into a stopper bead by going back through it from the tail end. Leave a 4"-6" (10cm-15cm) tail.

Pick up three main color beads and another accent bead. Repeat until there are a total of five accent beads and five groups of main color beads. Go through the second accent bead you picked up in the direction of the tail.

Earring pattern 2

Weave up the next three main color beads and the first accent bead (1). Pick up three main color beads, one accent bead and three more main color beads. Go through the accent bead that sticks out (2).

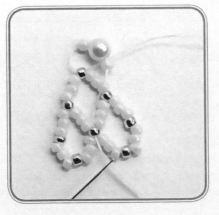

Earring pattern 3

Pick up three main color beads, one accent bead, three main color beads, one accent bead and three more main color beads. Go up through the accent bead that was added in pattern 2.

Earring pattern 4

Weave a working thread up to the tip of the triangle and go through the accent bead. Pick up one main color bead, one 4mm bead and one main color bead. Go through the accent bead that is in a vertical line below the tip accent bead.

Earring pattern 5

Weave over to the accent bead on the bottom of the triangle. Pick up one main color bead, one 4mm bead and one more main color bead. Go through the accent bead that is in a vertical line above it.

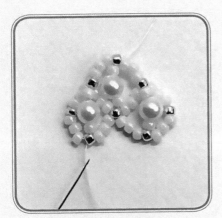

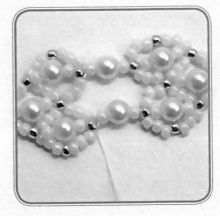

Earring pattern 6

Repeat earring pattern 5 on the other side of the triangle.

Repeat earring pattern 1–6 to make three more triangles.

Earring assembly 1

Weave a working thread so it is coming out of one of the bottom accent beads. Pick up one main color bead, one 4mm bead and one main color bead. Go through the corresponding accent bead of another triangle.

Go back through the main color bead, the 4mm bead and the next main color bead. Go through the accent bead the thread originally exited from on the opposite side.

Earring assembly 2

Weave over to the next accent bead on the bottom of the triangle and repeat the connecting beads pattern from earring assembly 1.

Repeat earring assembly 1–2 with the remaining two triangles.

Earring assembly 3

Repeat flower drop pattern 1–3 from
the Tiara Necklace (see page 124) to
make one flower drop.

Using the circle stitch, attach one
flower drop to the tip accent bead
of the triangle piece (see photo for
placement). Repeat this step with the
other earring.

Earring assembly 4

Weave a working thread so it is
coming out of the top accent bead of
the top triangle of an earring. Pick up
five main color beads. Go through the
loop of the earwire and back through
the tip accent bead on the opposite
side from where the thread originally
exited. Reinforce.

Repeat this step on the other
earring.

LACY FLOWER NECKLACE

I am drawn to asymmetrical designs and shapes. I am not a very mathematical person, and my work often comes about because of happy accidents rather than precise planning. This necklace reflects that asymmetrical side of me. Because the flowers are made separately, they can be used for stand-alone pieces, like pins and earrings, or you can make a whole bunch for your very own beaded garden.

Materials

size 12 beading needle

size D Nymo thread

tweny-six 4mm bicone crystals

five drop beads

one 10mm round bead

six 4mm round beads

12 grams size 11 Japanese seed beads for main color

2 grams size 15 Japanese seed beads for main color

4 grams size 15 Japanese seed beads for accent color

   TWO STARS

Flower pattern 1

Start with 1yd. (1m) of thread, single thickness with no knot. Pick up five 4mm crystals and go back through all five crystals again from the tail end. Leave a 4"–6" (10cm–15cm) tail.

Go through one more crystal to pull the circle tighter.

Flower pattern 2

Pick up fourteen size 15 main color beads. Go back through the crystal the thread is exiting from on the opposite side. This creates a loop around the crystal.

Flower pattern 3

Pick up seven size 15 accent beads and go back through the same crystal again on the opposite side. This creates a smaller loop that should sit on top of the larger loop.

Flower pattern 4

Weave up to the first three beads of the main color (large) loop. Pick up three size 15 accent beads and go through the third main color bead that your thread is exiting from on the opposite side. This creates a picot.

Go through the next three beads of the main color loop and create another three bead picot with the accent color.

Repeat this step two more times, for a total of four picots.

Flower pattern 5

Go through the last two size 15 beads of the main color loop. Go through the crystal. Go through the next crystal.

Repeat flower pattern 2–5, weaving over to the next crystal after finishing each petal, until you have a petal on each crystal. (There should be five petals.) Weave in the tail thread and the working thread.

Repeat flower pattern 1–5 to make two more flowers, for a total of three on the necklace.

Flower pattern 6

Follow flower pattern 1–3, weaving over to the next crystal after finishing each petal, to make one flower without the picots. This will be used later as a beadcap.

Weave the tail thread and the working thread in and tie them off.

Chain pattern 1

Start a new thread, approximately 2yd. (2m) long, single thickness with no knot. Pick up one size 15 accent bead and turn it into a stopper bead by going back through it from the tail end. Leave a 10"–12" (25cm–30cm) tail.

Pick up eight size 11 main color beads, one size 15 accent bead and one size 11 main color bead. Go back through the seventh size 11 main color bead. This creates a picot with the size 15 bead at the tip.

Chain pattern 2

Pick up one size 11 main color bead, skip the next bead and go through the next one. Repeat two more times. The thread should now be coming out of the first size 11 main color bead.

Chain pattern 3

Pick up two size 15 accent beads and go down through the size 11 main color bead that is sticking out (it is actually the last bead picked up in the previous step). This is the turnaround to go back down the beadwork.

Chain pattern 4

Pick up one size 11 main color bead and go through the next bead that is sticking out. Repeat two more times. This should bring the thread out of the bottom size 11 bead.

Chain pattern 5

Pick up two size 11 main color beads, one of the size 15 accent beads and then one more size 11 main color bead. Go up through the first size 11 bead that was picked up. This creates a picot. Pull this snug against the other beads.

Chain pattern 6

Pick up one size 11 main color bead and go up through the bead that is sticking out. Repeat two more times.

Chain pattern 7

Pick up three size 15 accent beads and go back down through the size 11 bead that is sticking out (it is the last size 11 bead just added).

Chain pattern 8

Pick up one size 11 bead and go through the next bead that is sticking out. Repeat two more times. The thread should now be coming out of the bottom size 11 bead.

Repeat chain pattern 5–8 until the beadwork is the desired length for the necklace. A good average length is 17¹/₂" (44cm).

Chain pattern 9

Put the needle on the tail thread left earlier. It should be coming out of the size 15 accent bead that was a stopper bead. Pick up one size 11 main color bead, one 4mm round bead, and three size 15 accent beads. Skip the accent beads and go back down the 4mm round bead and the size 11 bead. Reinforce.

Chain pattern 10

Put the needle on the working thread on the other end of the beadwork. Weave the thread so it is coming out of one of the size 11 beads at the end of the necklace. Pick up enough size 11 beads to fit comfortably but snugly around the 4mm bead. Go through a size 11 bead on the other side of the necklace. Reinforce.

Fringe assembly 1

To create the first fringe, weave the working thread on the loop side of the necklace so it is coming out of the seventh single size 15 accent bead from the end on the bottom edge of the band. The thread should be going in the direction of the loop.

Pick up three size 11 main color beads, one 4mm crystal, three size 11 beads, one drop bead and three size 11 beads. Skip the last three size 11 beads and go back up the remaining beads. Go through the size 15 accent bead at the top on the opposite side that the thread exited.

Fringe assembly 2

To create the second fringe, weave over to the fourth size 15 accent bead from the end.

Pick up three size 11 main color beads, one 4mm round bead, three size 11 beads, one 4mm crystal, three size 11 beads, one drop bead and three size 11 beads. Skip the last three size 11 beads and go back up the remaining beads. Go through the size 15 accent bead at the top, on the opposite side from where the thread originally exited.

Fringe assembly 3

To create the center fringe, weave the thread down to the first size 15 accent bead on the bottom edge of the band.

Pick up three of the size 11 main color beads, one 4mm crystal, three size 11 beads and one 4mm round bead. Go through the center opening of the flower without any picots (it will make a beadcap over the 10mm bead).

Pick up the 10mm bead, one size 11 bead, one 4mm crystal, one size 11 bead, one drop bead and three size 11 beads. Skip the last three size 11 beads and go back up the remaining beads.

Fringe assembly 4

On the clasp bead end of the necklace, make a fringe on the first size 15 accent bead that mirrors the second fringe created on the first side, as instructed in fringe assembly 2.

Weave over to the fourth size 15 accent bead and repeat the first fringe, as instructed in fringe assembly 1.

Fringe assembly 5

Weave a working thread so it is coming out of the center of the band in between the two fringes.

Go through the center opening on one of the picot flowers, pick up one 4mm round bead and three size 15 accent beads. Skip the three accent beads and go back down the round bead and the center opening of the flower. Go through the bead of the band again to secure the flower. Reinforce.

Fringe assembly 6

Attach the other two picot flowers to the other side of the band in the same way as described in fringe assembly 5. One flower should be at the end, and the other flower should be next to it.

Tie off any remaining threads.

THREE
STRAND
BRACELET

This bracelet is light and delicate, and it doesn't require many materials. It would make a great present for all of your friends—after you make one for yourself, of course!

Materials

size 12 beading needle

size D Nymo thread

six 3mm bicone crystals

six 4mm bicone crystals

one 12mm crystal rivoli

two 6mm rondelle beads

7 grams size 15 Japanese seed beads for main color

2 grams size 15 Japanese seed beads for accent color

TWO STARS ✦ ✦

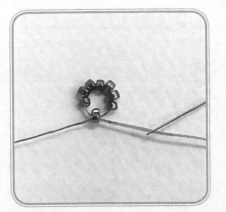

Chain pattern 1

Start with approximately 2yd. (2m) of thread, single thickness with no knot. Pick up one main color bead and turn it into a stopper bead by going back through it from the tail end. Leave a 6"–8" (15cm–20cm) tail.

Pick up seven main color beads and go back through the first bead (the stopper bead) from the tail end. Only go through the one bead. This makes a small circle. Pull snug.

Chain pattern 2

Pick up two main color beads. Go through the fifth bead of the original eight beads by going forward (skipping three beads), following the direction of the thread. Push the two new main color beads into the middle of the circle.

Chain pattern 3

Pick up six main color beads and go up through the bead that is below the bead that the thread is exiting from. Pull snug. The thread should be coming over the top of the beads.

Chain pattern 4

Pick up two main color beads and go up through the third bead of the six beads picked up in pattern 3. The two new beads should sit in the center of the circle. Make sure the thread is always coming out of the top of the beads.

Repeat chain pattern 3-4 until the chain is the desired length. A good approximate length is 6¹/2" (16cm) long. (The ends of the chain should just meet around your wrist. When the crystal clasp is added, it adds the necessary length for the proper fit.)

Notice that as the chain progresses, there will be two beads on each edge of the chain that stick out. Also notice that the chain basically consists of a circle (or square) with eight beads, two on each side with two beads in the middle of each circle.

Chain pattern 5

After the first chain is the desired length, you add the second chain. Start a new thread approximately 2yd. (2m) long, single thickness with no knot. Pick up one main color bead and turn it into a stopper bead by going back through it from the tail end.

Pick up one main color bead. Go through the first two beads on the side of the first chain at the tail end.

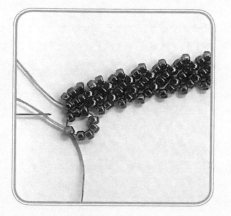

Chain pattern 6

Pick up four main color beads. Go back through the stopper bead from the tail end. This makes a small circle that is attached to the first chain.

Chain pattern 7

Pick up two main color beads and go through the first bead of the four from pattern 6.

Go through the next two side beads of the first chain.

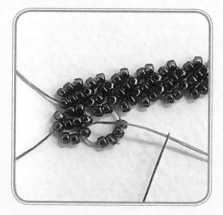

Chain pattern 8

Pick up four main color beads and go up through the bead below the one that the thread is exiting from.

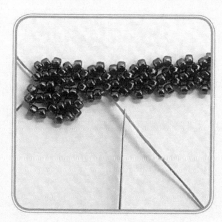

Chain pattern 9

Pick up two main color beads and go through the first bead of the four beads from pattern 8.

Go through the next two beads of the first chain. There should now be two circles of the second chain connected to the first chain.

Chain pattern 10

Pick up four main color beads and go up through the bead that is below the bead that the thread is exiting from.

Chain pattern 11

Pick up two main color beads and go through the first bead of the four beads from step 10. Do not Go through the next two side beads.

The first two chains are now connected by the first three circles.

Chain pattern 12

Pick up six main color beads and go up through the bead that is below the bead the thread originally exited from.

Chain pattern 13

Pick up two main color beads and go up through the third bead of the six beads from pattern 12.

Repeat chain pattern 12–13 until the second chain is three circles shorter than the first chain.

Chain pattern 14

To make sure the second chain is three circles shorter than the first chain, lay it alongside the first chain and either count or line up the two bead groups along the edge.

To start connecting the last three circles, go through the two side beads of the first chain (third set from the end) after your last circle on the second chain.

Chain pattern 15

Pick up four main color beads and go up through the bead that is below the one that the thread is exiting from.

Chain pattern 16

Pick up two main color beads and go through the first bead of the four from step 15. Go through the next two beads of the first chain.

Chain pattern 17

Repeat repeat chain pattern 15–16 to connect the two chains.

Start a new thread, approximately 2yd. (2m) long, single thickness with no knot.

Follow chain pattern 5–16 to add the third and final chain section. Leave the working threads attached for now.

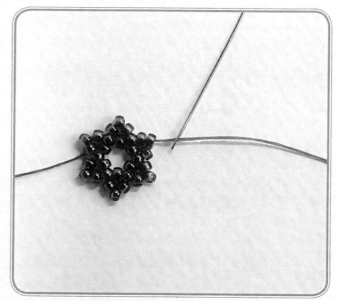

Flower pattern 1

Start a new thread approximately 2yd. (2m) long, single thickness with no knot. Pick up twelve accent beads and go back through all of them again from the tail end. Needle forward through one more bead. This creates a small circle. Leave a 4"–6" (10cm–15cm) tail.

Flower pattern 2

Pick up three accent beads, skip over a bead and go through the next bead of the original circle. Repeat five more times. This makes six points around the original circle.

After the sixth point is added, go through the first two bead of the first point. This brings the working thread out of the middle bead of the point and lines it up for the next row of points.

Flower pattern 3

Pick up five accent beads and go through the middle bead of the next point from the previous row. (It will be the second bead of the point.) Repeat five more times.

After the sixth point is added, go through the first three beads of the first point of this row.

Flower pattern 4

Pick up seven accent beads and go through the middle bead of the point from the previous row. (It will be the third bead of the point.) Repeat five more times.

After the sixth point is added, go through the first four beads of the first point of this row.

Flower pattern 5

Pick up four accent beads and go through the middle bead of the point from the previous row. (It will be the fourth bead of the point.) Pull this snug. The beadwork will start to pull in. Repeat five more times.

After the sixth point, put the crystal inside the netting and pull snug. Reinforce this row one time.

Flower pattern 6

The working thread should be coming out of the fourth bead of a point from the row with seven beads per point. (These are the beads that are slightly recessed from the last row of the netting.) Pick up one 4mm crystal and one accent bead. Skip the accent bead and go back down the crystal.

Go through the point bead the thread originally exited from on the opposite side. Pull snug.

Flower pattern 7

Pick up one accent bead, one 3mm crystal and one accent bead. Go through the next middle (fourth) bead of the row with seven beads per point. (These are the beads that are slightly recessed from the last row of the netting.)

Flower pattern 8

Repeat flower pattern 6-7 until you have gone all the way around the netting. There should be six 4mm crystals and six 3mm crystals around the netting.

If the crystals feel a little loose, go back and reinforce them. Tie off the tail thread but leave the working thread.

Bracelet assembly 1

There should be threads on each end of the chain. Pick the longest thread on one end and tie off the rest.

At the end of the chain, there are three groups of two beads. Weave the working thread so it is coming out of the first bead of the two beads of one of the groups on the top or bottom.

Go through a middle point bead (the third bead) of a point on the row of netting with five point beads. Go back through the end bead on the end of the chain that the thread originally exited from on the opposite side. Reinforce.

x

Bracelet assembly 2

Weave the thread to the middle point bead (the third bead) of the next point on the row of netting with five point beads.

Go through the first (inside) bead of the other set of two beads on the top or bottom of the chain. Reinforce.

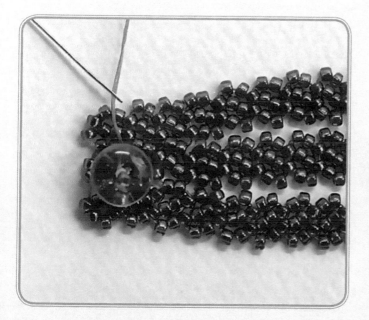

Bracelet assembly 4

On the other end of the chain, weave in all but the longest thread. Then weave the longest thread so it is coming out of the middle set of two beads that are slightly inside the chain. Again, if you can't find the exact set of two beads, just center the thread in the chain slightly in from the end. Also, make sure you are on the right side of the chain.

Pick up one accent bead, one 6mm rondelle bead and one accent bead. Skip the last accent bead and go back down the rondelle bead and the accent bead. Go through the bead of the chain that the thread originally exited from on the opposite side. Reinforce.

Weave in the thread and tie it off.

Bracelet assembly 3

Weave the thread so it is coming out of the middle set of two beads that are slightly inside the chain. The thread should be on the same side as the front of the crystal clasp. If you can't find the set of two beads, just center the thread in the chain slightly away from the crystal clasp.

Pick up one 6mm rondelle bead and one accent bead. Skip the accent bead and go back down the rondelle. Go back through the bead of the chain that the thread originally exited from on the opposite side. Reinforce.

Bracelet assembly 5

Put a needle on the working thread left earlier on the netting of the crystal. Weave it so it is coming out of the middle (second) bead of the netting row that has three beads per point. It should also be the middle point bead that is across from where the chain is connected to the netting.

Pick up enough accent beads to fit comfortably but snugly around the rondelle bead. Go back through the point bead the thread originally exited from on the opposite side. Reinforce.

Tie off any remaining threads.

Resources

The tools and materials used in this book are available at your loca bead store or craft store. For more information on the products used, contact these manufactures:

BERKELY FISHING
www.berkley-fishing.com
FireLine

TOHO CO., LTD.
www.tohobeads.net
One-G thread

NEW BEDFORD THREAD CO., INC.
www.newbedfordthread.com
Silamide

THREAD HEAVEN
www.threadheaven.com
Thread Heaven thread conditioner and protectant

MIYUKI CO. LTD.
www.miyuki-beads.co.jp/english
Delica beads

OTTLITE
www.ottlite.com
True-light task lamps

Index

FALL IN LOVE WITH THESE TITLES FROM NORTH LIGHT BOOKS AND KRAUSE PUBLICATIONS

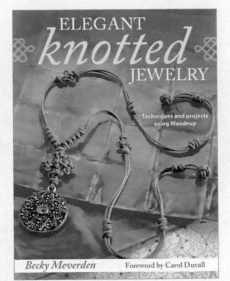

Beaded Colorways
by Beverly Ash Gilbert

Beyond Beading Basics
by Carole Rodgers

Elegant Knotted Jewelry
by Becky Meverden

Learn to approach color as a painter does, only your palette will be rainbow-hued beads, and your paintings will be spectacular jewelry you can wear! *Beaded Colorways* shows you how to mix beads and gems together to create custom color blends called Bead Soups. These "soups" are then woven together into 18 dazzling pieces that are more like works of art than simple jewelry. You'll even learn how to seamlessly stitch from one color to another, helping you create stunning multicolor jewelry.

Take your beading skills to the next level as you go *Beyond Beading Basics*. Conquer the more complex aspects of beading, such as using common bead findings as integral parts of your designs, using multiple-hole beads, making baskets and other shapes with wire and beads and how to combine stitches to achieve unique effects. Carole Rodgers offers you more than 25 projects and an equal number of techniques to launch you into bead artistry.

Now you can discover the beautiful, traditional craft of maedeup, as you create gorgeous jewelry projects using colorful cording and beads. Author Becky Meverden first shows you how to create the knots themselves, then how to use them in projects from a simple pair of knotted earrings to an intricate dragonfly necklace and a modern wire plus cord watch. *Elegant Knotted Jewelry* includes everything you'll need to know to create your own maedeup jewelry

ISBN-10: 1-60061-318-7
ISBN-13: 978-1-60061-318-0
128 pages, paperback, Z2925

ISBN-10: 0-89689-925-X
ISBN-13: 978-0-89689-925-4
144 pages, paperback, Z3628

ISBN-10: 0-89689-818-0
ISBN-13: 978-0-89689-818-9
128 pages, paperback, Z2955

These and other fine North Light and Krause Publication titles are available from your local craft retailer, bookstore or online retailer, or visit out Web site a www.mycraftivitystore.com.

Made in the USA
San Bernardino, CA
25 May 2014